The

Power of Agape Love

The

Power of Agape Love

by Dr. Juanita Crawford, *Ed.D, MSN, RN*

Senior Publisher
Steven Hill

ASA Publishing Corporation

A Publisher Trademark Title page

ASA Publishing Corporation
An Accredited Publishing House with the BBB

105 E. Front St., Suite 101
Monroe, Michigan 48161
www.asapublishingcorporation.com

Copyrights©2016 Juanita Crawford, All Rights Reserved
Title: The Power of Agape Love
Date Published: 05.14.2016 / Edition 1 *Trade Paperback*
Book ID: ASAPCID2380697
ISBN: 978-0692717585
Library of Congress Cataloging-in-Publication Data

This book was published in the United States of America.
State of Michigan

A Publisher Trademark Copy page

"THE POWER OF AGAPE LOVE"

Acknowledging God's Authentic Power Everyday (AGAPE)

by

Dr. Juanita Crawford, Ed.D, MSN, RN

Who can define a surpassed meaning of true love except God who is Love? (1 John 4:8). For God so Love the world that He gave His Only Begotten Son (John 3: 16) Jesus Christ. God commands each and every one of us to exchange love, "A new commandment I give unto you, that ye love one another; as I have loved you, that ye also love one another. By this shall all men know that ye are my disciples, if ye have love one to another" (John 13:34-35). Certainly, no love is more powerful than Agape Love.

FORWARD

LOVE IS THE GREATEST GIFT OF ALL (1ST CORINTHIANS 13:13); YET MANY INDIVIDUALS OF THE WORLD HAVE BECOME DESENSITIZED TO OTHERS' FEELINGS. ONE MAY ASK, WHAT DOES LOVE HAVE TO DO WITH ANYTHING? MY ANSWER, LOVE IS SIGNIFICANT IN EVERY ASPECT OF OUR LIVES. FOR IT WAS LOVE THAT CAUSE GOD TO SEND HIS ONE AND ONLY BEGOTTEN SON JESUS CHRIST TO THE OLD RUGGED CROSS (ROMANS 5:8). LEST WE FORGET, WITHOUT THE LOVE OF OUR LORD AND SAVIOR JESUS CHRIST AND THE SHEDDING OF HIS INNOCENT BLOOD, THERE WOULD BE NO FORGIVENESSS OF OUR SINS (HEBREWS 9:22) OR REDEMPTION OF OUR SOULS (PSALMS 111:9).

THIS IS AUTHENTICATION OF THE POWER OF AGAPE LOVE!

DEDICATION

This book is dedicated to my parents the late Rev. and Mrs. Thomas Ford who instilled love and gratitude in my heart, and to my entire family. May God Bless and Keep you all in His everlasting Love!

The Ford Family

Bottom Front Row (Left to Right): Theresa, Wanda (sitting on Dad), David, and Juanita. **Second Row** (Left to Right): Willie Thomas, Rev. Thomas Ford Sr. (Dad), Mae Frances Ford (Mom), and Cornelius. **Back Row** (Left to Right): Rebecca, Ann, and Gwendolyn.

Vertical (Right Side): Mark, Demetrius and Jonathan. As quoted in the Word of God, and was often spoken by my father *"Let brotherly love continue"* (Hebrews 13:1).

ACKNOWLEDGEMENTS

I give reverence to my Lord and Savior Jesus Christ for allowing me to write my 2nd book. *Heavenly Father, Thank you for providing God fearing parents who taught me about my Lord and Savior Jesus Christ, for imbedding the importance of loving one another in my heart, and for allowing me to gain insight, foresight, and hindsight regarding the significance of Agape Love.* To my husband (Rev. Emmett Crawford Jr.), thank you for proof-reading and editing.

All Scriptures quoted and paraphrased are taken from the Holy Bible (KJV), unless otherwise denoted

TABLE OF CONTENTS

The

Power of Agape Love

by Dr. Juanita Crawford, *Ed.D, MSN, RN*

CHAPTER 1
INTRODUCTION

Misconception of Love

The word Love has been misconstrued by many in our society, in particular our youth.   In past times love was meticulously taught in our homes especially concerning the love of God.   Parents were more God-fearing and obedient to the Word of God and trained their children up in the way that they should go (Godly) for remembrance in the days of old (Proverbs 22:6). Children were taken to church by their parents (not sent) and at the age in which their intellect and decision making processes were developed, freely they joined the church, and turned their lives over to Jesus Christ, to cleanse them of their sins.   In addition to parents teaching their children about the love of God and the rewards that comes in being obedient to His Word, spiritual leaders (ministers, deacons, and Sunday school teachers), neighbors, relatives, and secular school teachers assisted in this effort.   What has happened to our parents in showing and implementing love?   What happened to the love we once showed toward one another in particular, Agape love?   One may ask, what is Agape love?   Before defining Agape love, let's first define the word love.

What is Love?

One philosopher asserts, "Love is the most powerful emotion a human being can experience. The strange thing is that almost nobody knows what love is" (Catron, 2015, p.1).   "Why is it so difficult to find love? That is easy to understand, if you know that the word *love* is not the same as one's feeling of love" (Catron, 2015, p.1). Philosopher Catron goes on to say, "The word love is used and abused for the expression of different sets of feelings. The word love is used as an expression of affection towards someone else (I love you) but it also expresses pleasure "I love chocolate" (Catron, 2015, p.1). According to Catron (2015), the word love also expresses a human virtue that is based on compassion, affection and kindness; this is a state of being that has nothing to do with something or someone outside yourself and is the purest form of Love. Philosopher Catron affirms various forms of love

Seven Forms of Love

Catron (2015) denotes the ancient Greek defined and employed the word love in *seven* different states:

Storge: natural affection, the love you share with your family. *Philia:* the love that you have for friends. *Eros:* sexual and erotic desire kind of love (positive or negative). *Agape:* this is the unconditional love, or divine love. *Ludus:* this is playful love, like childish love or flirting.

Pragma: long standing love, the love in a married couple. *Philautia:* the love of the self (negative or positive). These are *7 different kinds of feelings.* The love you feel for your partner is not the same as the love you feel for your mother. Even the love for your partner changes in time. You feel different emotions for different situations and people (p.1).

In congruent with Catron, Merriam-Webster (2015a) defines love as having a strong affection for another arising, out of kinship or personal ties. Philosopher Anapol (2011) on a personal note adds that "love is inherently free. It cannot be bought, sold, or traded. You cannot make someone love you, nor can you prevent it, for any amount of money" (p.1). Interestingly, he goes on to say that "Love cannot be imprisoned nor can it be legislated. Love is not a substance, not a commodity, nor even a marketable power source. Love has no territory, no borders, no quantifiable mass, or energy output" (Anapol, 2011, p.1). While these meanings are attention-grabbing, insightful, and true, we will now view the meaning of love from a religious perspective.

Wybourne (2015), a Benedictine nun posit:
Love is more easily experienced than defined. As a theological virtue, by which we love God above all things and our neighbors as ourselves for his sake, it seems remote until we encounter it enfleshed, so to say, in the life of another – in acts of kindness, generosity and *self-sacrifice.* Love's the one thing that can never hurt anyone, although it may cost dearly. The

paradox of love is that it is supremely free yet attaches us with bonds stronger than death. It cannot be bought or sold; there is nothing it cannot face; love is life's greatest blessing (p.1).

There are various worldwide perspectives and definitions of the word love. However, perspectives of storge, philia, and eros love in relationship to dominating our society in good and bad ways will be the focus of the literature enclosed in comparison to Agape love. Now let us take a glance at Storge love.

CHAPTER 2
FAMILY FOUNDATION

Storge Love

Storge is a Greek word (Στοργή) and refers to natural affection parents have for their children (Wikipedia, 2013). While both parents *may* love their children, it is the mother who initiates this bond with the child that starts in utero. Mothers are given the major role of caring, training, and chastising their children as noted in the Bible in Proverbs 29:15 (NIV), "A rod and a reprimand impart wisdom, but a child left undisciplined disgraces its mother." Why have we allowed lawmakers to stop us from chastising our children? Henry (2015) argues, "The undutiful behavior of children towards their parents is a very great provocation to God our common Father; and, if men do not punish it, he will" (p.4). Why are mothers leaving the home (instead of raising their children) taking on leadership roles (now head of household) and our men staying at home to babysit? Even more, why are we not protecting our children from violence, molestation, and death? Have we become self-centered, impatient, immoral and worldly; yet we say we are Christians, we are the church, we are the body of Christ, and we love God, but are not obedient to His Word. Furthermore, where are the fathers of our beloved children? Fathers are missing in the homes and some mothers have become demonized with no concept of storge love.

Mothers are killing their children in a mighty way. Orenstein (2014) found that in the past 32 years in the United States alone at least one parent murders their child and it happens about 500 times a year, while Goad (2014) found that an estimated 200 children are murdered annually by their mothers who may be sent to a mental institution versus a prison. Not only are mothers killing their children, but so are fathers who are held lawfully in higher regards. A "1969 study conducted by Dr. Phillip Resnick found that when mothers kill their kids, 68% are sent to mental hospitals and only 27% are sent to prison; yet when fathers kill their children, 72% go to prison and only 14% are hospitalized" (Goad, 2014, p.1). Is not murder, murder regardless of who commits it?

What happened to parents providing homes as safe havens for their beloved children? *Storge love* for some mothers and fathers have undoubtedly waxed cold. When children are not being murdered by their parents they are being molested (Dolan, 2013; Shen, 2012), not just by fathers but by other males in general. In fact, approximately one in twenty adolescent males and adult men sexually abuse children. *Have mercy Lord!* Research found in 1998 alone there were approximately 103,000 cases (reported and confirmed) of child molestation in the United States (Child

Molestation Research & Prevention Institute, 2015). Currently in the United States, more than three million children are victims struggling with molestation. Even worse, many prefer to struggle alone with their molestation issues because they feel no other adults will help them (Child Molestation Research & Prevention Institute, 2015). Heartbreaking, so many children never experience storge love in their homes.

Moreover, many mothers are aware of their children molestations, but often fear for their own well-being from the molesters (be it husbands or boyfriends). Our society is in grave need of God-fearing parents, in particular men to restore storge and Agape love to our children, who were given to us as a gift from God (Psalm 127:3). What happened to the prudent men in our society, for "wise man feareth, and departeth from evil; but the fool rageth, and is confident" (Proverbs 14:16). Men in representing God's glory must come back to God, turn from their wicked ways, and return to their homes for effective parental structure and the epitomizing of storge love.

Men, God's Glory

A father holds a great responsibility in loving, caring, and providing for his wife and children. The love that a man holds for his wife should be as stated in Ephesians 5:25, "Husbands, love your wives, even as Christ also loved the church, and gave himself for it" and in showing storge love for their children should not ". . . exasperate your children; instead, bring them up in the training and instruction of the Lord (Ephesians 6:

4, NIV). Motionless men have become stiff-necked, lacking love for their children, have departed from God, and are not only abusing but killing their wives (KHQ, 2013; Mills, 1994). Internationally, roughly 40 percent of females are murdered by their former/present spouse or male significant other, who claimed they killed them because they loved them too much (Ben-Zeev, 2014). Where is the Agape love? Storge love in our society has diminished even to the point of one killing the entire family, help us Lord! Familicide is rampaging in our society.

Recently a 29 year old Utah man killed his wife (26), two children (ages 6, 2), and then himself on Father's Day (Parker, 2015). In Texas, a 49 year old male broke into his ex's girlfriend's home, killed her (40), her husband (50), and her six children ages: 13, 11, 10, 9, 7, and 6. Howbeit, the 13 year old child he murdered was his own biological son (Wagner & Hensley, 2015). With all the hatred exemplified between mothers and fathers in our homes (instead of storge love), how can we expect our children to love one another? All children are vulnerable to environmental influences, nevertheless are still held accountable to God.

Yes, although storge love is not present in the homes of our children, God still holds children accountable in respecting their parents. Colossians 3:20 states, "Children, obey your parents in everything, for this pleases the Lord." In spite of how they are reared up they still have a responsibility to God and must "obey your parents in the Lord, for this is right. Honor your father and mother which is the first commandment with a promise, so that it may go well with you and that you may enjoy long life on the earth" (Ephesians 6: 1-3, NIV). Unfortunately, children reared up in sin-sick environments become the product of their environment and when their parents elicit violence and hatred towards their children they become desensitized to love for their parents. This desensitization results in anger and the absence of storge love for their parents. In fact, some children rebel against their parents to the point of suing them (Draper, 2013; Schmadeke, 2011) while others go to the extreme of killing them without remorse. *Help us Lord!*

On Easter Sunday (2011) in the United Kingdom, a 14 year old boy sneaks into his mother's room, smashes her head with a claw hammer after mowing the lawn and starts eating chocolate. The child then covered his mother with paper, poured gasoline on her, and set her on fire. According to a reporter, the child became very disturbed and developed behavioral problems after his mother divorced the child's father when he was nine years old (The Richest, 2015). In 2006 in Medicine Hat, Alberta, Canada, a 12 year old girl and her 23 year old boyfriend (23) brutally stabbed her mother, father, and eight year old brother to death so that they could run off together. The father was stabbed so badly that there was little blood left in his body (The Richest, 2015).

In 2003 a 16 year old girl killed her parents (father 46, mother 52) because they did not approve of her 19 year old boyfriend (Montaldo, 2015a), and in 2001 in Escambia County, Florida, two brothers (12 and

13 years of age) bludgeoned their 40 year old father to death by cracking his skull open and smashing in his face with an aluminum baseball bat. The two brothers then set the house on fire in hopes of covering up the murder (Montaldo, 2015b). The brothers' rationales for killing their father were; they did not want to be punished for running away (prior to them killing their father; yet, they stated their dad never hit them), and they did not like the way their dad stared at them (they called this mental abuse) when he made them sit in a room (Montaldo, 2015b).

What has become of true storge love in our families? As a society one could argue that we have bulldozed *Storge* love (natural affection, the love you share with your family), denounced *Pragma* love (long standing love, the love in a married couple), and have become sensitized and bottled-up in Philautia love (love of self, negative or positive) as defined by (Catron, 2015). In agreement with Catron (2015) it's apparent that society is misconstrued with what love is and what love is not. For the most part, in the above instances, love has been cast aside causing one's heart to become discontent and filled with hatred. Still God is a forgiving God that can restore love to the broken hearted. Only divine love makes one content, and it must stem from the heart as will be defined in *Agape love*. In defining true love, one must turn to the originator of love: God. One could challenge that society in returning to the days of old (dependent on God) in which saints came together, worshipped and trusted God, exhibited love in their hearts for one another, and forgave each other, will experience a better outcome in one's relationship with their spouses and children. Often we hear the saying; it takes a village to raise a child, is there truth to this assertion?

While many believe it takes a village to raise our children some believe the true foundation in effectively raising children begins in the home with charity and meticulous upbringing from both parents. In my humble opinion, effectively raising children takes God-fearing righteousness parents and *strong individuals in their environment who have the love of God* in their hearts and the children's best interest at heart. One author (Berkley, 1997), expounding on it takes a village to raise our children found; *it takes a sense of obligation and respect toward God.* Although some of our children's desires may be granted, as our commitment to please God and our decision to take on parenthood, we are responsible and must tend to their basic needs. Except the Lord build the house, they labor in vain that build it," (Psalm 127:1).

(Berkley, 1997), goes on to say it takes love: parents should establish strong bonds and natural affection of love for their children, unlike no other. Without this affection parents will have little power in raising their children (Romans: 1:31). Children need both parents to render love and raise them (Titus 2:4). The author attest it *takes moral conviction*: We must not let our children act out in their youth displaying disobedience, disrespect, or rebellious behaviors (Berkley, 1997). Parents tolerating children's rebellious behaviors signify no moral courage, and only further escalation of rebellious behaviors. Parents have a moral obligation *first to God* in not tolerating such behaviors and must pray diligently while setting high standards and resisting lawlessness which produces obedient and respectable children (Berkley, 1997).

In raising our children, it *takes patience*: Parents must develop patience and not readily give-up or assume the worst on the behalf of their children. Just as God forgives and changes adults (after we repent), He does likewise with children. Furthermore, not all parents are effective or correct in training up their children (Berkley, 1997). The Word reminds us, "Fathers, do not provoke your children, lest they become discouraged" (Colossians 3:21). The author further states in effectively raising children, *it takes the influence of Godly examples*. Children generally mimic the behaviors' in their surroundings. In fact, Apostle Paul remembered the faith of Timothy and spoke of the influence of his God-fearing mother and grandmother regarding his upbringing (Berkley, 1997).

Paul commended (2nd Tim. 1:5 and 2nd Tim. 3:15) Timothy's faith in stating, " . . . which dwelt first in your grandmother Lois and your mother Eunice, and I am persuaded in you also . . . that from childhood you have known the Holy Scriptures, which are able to make you wise for salvation through faith which is in Christ Jesus." I strongly concur with this author; society needs more God-fearing parents, grandparents, aunts, uncles, relatives, neighbors, and sincere friends to instill the teachings and love of God in our children's hearts while rearing them up. We need more love toward one another in our homes, schools, churches, and villages.

Love is highly needed in keeping each of us near to God, close-knit in our families, secure in our homes, safe in our schools, and out of prison cells. Men as God's Glory (1st Corinthians 11:7) are to be the stronghold as head of the family, yet they are *missing in action* in most homes. Unfortunately, we are living in a society that loves "the glory that comes from man more than the Glory that comes from God" (John 12:43, ESV). Let us all return to our First Love (God) and be obedient to His statures in training up our children righteously and effectively (both parents), for a "wise son brings joy to his father, but a foolish son brings grief to his mother" (Proverbs 10:1, NIV). Society is in great need of God-fearing parents in our homes.

The Significance of Both Parents in the Home

Many parents have left their homes or were never present in the home, in fact over the past decade the presence of both parents in the home with children decreased considerably. Although "the country added 160,000 families with children, the number of two-parent households decreased by 1.2 million. Fifteen million U.S. children (or 1 in 3), live without a father, and nearly 5 million live without a mother. In 1960, just 11 percent of American children lived in homes without fathers . . . the spiral continues each year. Married couples with children have an average income of $80,000, compared with $24,000 for single mothers" (Rosiak, 2012, p.1). The love of both parents is needed in our homes, particular from the fathers.

"There is a father factor in nearly all of the

social issues facing America today. But the hope lies in the fact that children with involved fathers do better across every measure of child well-being than their peers in father-absent homes" (National Fatherhood Initiative, 2014). One study conducted on father involvement with 134 children of adolescent mothers over the first 10 years of life contends children who are more interactive with their father's experience fewer behavior problems and score higher on reading achievement (Howard, Lefever, Borkowski, & Whitman, 2006). According to the U.S. Department of Health & Human Services (2012), "Children in father-absent homes are almost four times more likely to be poor. In 2011, twelve percent of children in married families were living in poverty; compared to 44 percent of children in mother-only families" (p.1).

One study (2,111 respondents) conducted regarding fathers absent in the home, in relationship to emotional and behavioral problems, examined the prevalence of mothers' relationship changes from birth to 3 years of age. Results revealed that children born to single mothers showed higher levels of aggressive behavior, than children born to married mothers. Results showed living in a single-mother home is comparable to experiencing 5.25 partnership changeovers (Osborne & McLanahan, 2007). In 1998 Statistics exposed, "infant mortality rates were 1.8 times higher for infants of unmarried mothers" (Matthews, Curtin, & MacDormann, 2000, p. 6).

Harper and McLanahan (2004) argued that in single mother's homes (with sustained income), youth incarcerations were significantly higher than in homes of youths with both parents. In addition, statistics show that there is significantly more drug and alcohol abuse among children who do not live with both parents in the home (Hoffmann, 2002). Nord and West (2001) found when fathers are involved in their children studies at school; their children tend to get higher academic grades (mostly A's) regardless if they were their biological fathers or stepfathers. Nevertheless, fatherless homes remain prevalent and mothers nationwide continue to strive vigorously in raising their children, and in most cases society highly regards them.

One can relate to this statement as noteworthy in the secular world in celebrating Mother's versus Father's Day. All around the world one can witness flowers and gifts by solicitors practically on every street corner during the week of Mother's day, while few to none are seen during the week of Father's day. According to a survey, 78 percent of respondents voiced if Mother's day and Father's day was on the same day, they would celebrate mothers. In fact, Mother's day has become the 3rd most celebrated holiday; 1st being Christmas, and 2nd Valentine's Day (Washington CBS Local, 2015). Truly, there are many single women who love their children and strive very hard to raise them up righteously; in fact, many of them tend to act more responsive in exhibiting storge to their children than Christians.

Indeed, credit must be given to single mothers (saved and unsaved) who strive hard in exhibiting storge love while raising their children. I am reminded of a harlot in the Bible who showed storge love for her child. As the story foretold, two harlots had recently given birth to their babies, one mother laid on her baby (mistakenly) and her baby died, so she switched the babies. After a defused argument between the two women the case was presented to King Solomon (known for his elite wisdom) for a resolution. The King after summoning the live baby to be cut in half with a sword, the true mother informed the king to let the other mother have the child (this was storge love).

King Solomon in all his wisdom now knew who the true mother was and rendered the baby to her (1st Kings 3: 16-28). With so much contention surrounding our society in relationship to storge love, how can one possibly have room in their heart for philia love? One can argue love must first be generated in self, our families, and our homes before we can love others. Dr. Greenberg (2012) posit, "Let us learn to love ourselves so we can be more open and compassionate to others, and so we can take down the walls that limit who we can be and what we can contribute" (p.1). Let us pray that God fill our hearts with *Agape Love* which incorporates storge love for our family and philia love for our neighbors (philia).

CHAPTER 3
LOVE THY NEIGHBOR

Philia Love

Philia being Greek (φιλία) is known as a friendship or brotherly love (Zavada, 2013). Incidentally, the Holy Bible teaches us to love one another, and as Christians in being obedient to Christ we are to obey His commandments. Yet, true love comes from God through our belief, faith and trust in Him; and by His Holy Spirit we are empowered and strengthen to love one another. Ephesians 3:15-17 (ESV) reminds us, "from whom every family in heaven and on earth is named, that according to the riches of his glory he may grant you to be strengthened with power through his Spirit in your inner being, so that Christ may dwell in your hearts through faith—that you, being rooted and grounded in love." Jesus speaks on the importance of philia (friendship) love in John 15: 14-17 stating:

> Ye are my friends, if ye do whatsoever I command you. Henceforth I call you not servants; for the servant knoweth not what his lord doeth: but I have called you friends; for all

things that I have heard of my Father I have made known unto you. Ye have not chosen me, but I have chosen you, and ordained you, that ye should go and bring forth fruit, and that your fruit should remain: that whatsoever ye shall ask of the Father in my name, he may give it you. These things I command you, that ye love one another.

Godly love will never give up or give out; in essence, charity never fails (1st Corinthians 13: 8). Genuine love for friends in today's society is very rare, for many equate love and friendship with the mentality of what's *in it for me?* "True friends should love at all times without dissemination" (Proverbs 17:7). Christians in spreading philia love are to treat all individuals with kindness (particularly other Christians), love, and respect. In fact, we owe it to our brothers and sisters to love one another. Paul in Romans 13:8, states, "Owe no man anything, but to love one another: for he that loveth another hath fulfilled the law." When showing love towards one another we must be mindful of what we say, and how we say it.

Often one may have a good message, but a bad method of presenting it, which in turn may hurt one's feelings. Speaking harsh words may provoke one to anger which may result in saying unpleasant things that can't be recanted. According to Mark 7: 20-23, ". . . that which cometh out of the man that defileth the man. For from within, out of the heart of men, proceed evil thoughts, adulteries, fornications, murders, thefts, covetousness, wickedness, deceit, lasciviousness, an evil eye, blasphemy, pride, foolishness: All these evil things come from within, and defile the man." God sees and hears all. We may get by, but we will not get away with mistreating others. Furthermore, we will not escape God's wrath; for all will reap what we sow (Galatians 6:7, *paraphrased*), no doubt about it.

Realistically speaking, Christians are not exempted from making mistakes in saying the wrong thing to others, in particular to new members of the fold. Have we spoken kind and encouraging words to each other, given them hope, prayed for them or shared love? Or, have we jumped on them about what they were wearing when they visited our church homes? My father used to say, *one has to catch a fish before they can clean it!* Have we forgotten how Christ accepted us in spite of the way we were dressed and regardless of our sinful nature? Still, Christ forgave us? Only God can change people and clean them up from the inside out. We must be careful in judging others and rid ourselves of the *holier than thou mentality:* for we all have faults and beams in our own eyes.

Matthew 7:3-5 expressively states, "And why beholdest thou the mote that is in thy brother's eye, but considerest not the beam that is in thine own eye? Or how wilt thou say to thy brother, let me pull out the mote out of thine eye; and, behold, a beam is in thine own eye? Thou hypocrite, first cast out the beam out of thine own eye; and then shalt thou see clearly to cast out the mote out of thy brother's eye." In fact, let us not be like the Pharisees in which Jesus rebuked in saying, "Now then, you Pharisees clean the outside of the cup and dish, but inside you are full of greed and wickedness (Luke 11:39).

Let us show love, plant strong seeds which will conquer all, and remove the negative vibes that are not preordained for the church of God. We must constantly pray and ask God to search our hearts for He is the only one that can see inside our hearts, remove imperfections, and change us to impersonate His nature (Agape Love) for the building up of His body. Proverbs 11:30 reminds us that, "The fruit of the righteous [is] a tree of life; and he that winneth souls [is] wise."

As Christians, we know that if meat offends our brother we should not eat it (Romans 14:21, 1 Corinthians 8:13), meaning we should not do anything that will cause our weaker brethren (in the Word and faith) to stumble. Yes, weaker brethrens have need for stronger Christians since they tend to be wise and knowledgeable. We as Christians must not become puffeth up thinking we are better. "But knowledge puffeth up is not good for nothing. We must conduct ourselves in a Godly fashion showing love and compassion toward our weaker brethren for... charity edifieth" (1st Corinthians 8:1). Christians in particular, must go to God for guidance in approaching our brethren, never in our own mind which falters and may possibly cause more harm than good in leading our weaker brethren to God.

Let us approach the weaker brethren with the love of God in our hearts while praying to not offend them; for we do not know everything. The Word of God confirms, "And if any man think that he knoweth any thing, he knoweth nothing yet as he ought to know. But if any man love God, the same is known of him (1st Corinthians 8:2-3). Christians in exhibiting *philia love* must "Let brotherly love continue. Be not forgetful to entertain strangers: for thereby some have entertained angels unawares" (Hebrews 13: 1). The conduct of Christians should be the emulation of Jesus (Agape Love), not hatred, or the showing of false love.

In reference to personal conduct in loving one another Leviticus 19: 17 states, "Thou shalt not hate thy brother in thine heart..." One must be mindful in displaying false love towards one another. If a man claims to love God and despiseth his brother in God's sight he is a liar. 1st John 4: 20 states, "For he that loveth not his brother whom he hath seen, how can he love God whom he hath not seen." Let us show Philia love towards one another which is demonstrated as heroic and powerful in devotion to a friend. Jesus stated in John 15: 13, "Greater love hath no man than this that a man lay down his life for his friends." *Have mercy Lord......are we our brother's keeper, for we all need each other.*

We Need Each Other

Everyone need and desires love and encouragements (philia love), regardless of who they are; at some point in time we will need someone to uplift our spirits, strengthen, and perhaps lend us a helping hand. In my humble opinion, The Word of God in Exodus 17:12 speaks of philia love when Moses, while standing on a hilltop holding up the rod of God with his outstretched hands needed assistance. Moses outstretched hands were assurance that Joshua and Israelites would win the war against the Amalekites (known as a repeated enemy of the Israelites) in Rephidim; yet, Moses hands became weary. Moses' hands were to remain steady (until the sun went down) as assurance from God the Israelites would win the battle, and whenever his hands became weary and leaned downward the Amaleks prevailed. Thank God for Aaron (Moses' brother) and Hur (Moses' brother-in-law; Miriam's' husband) who assisted in holding up Moses' hands (one on each side) keeping them steady until the sun set. God allowed Israel to triumph (Easton Bible Dictionary, n.d.; Exodus 17:12).

We as Christians must come together and stand up for our brothers and sisters in Christ. Let us also be concerned as to what type of Christian leadership they are being fed. We must put away the *don't care* attitude and show some gratitude and appreciation to our Lord and Savior by emulating Him. As Christians we should have more compassion in our hearts towards others regardless of their circumstances, for we are to imitate Christ. Jesus showed compassion for many individuals while traveling from one place to another and helped them with various needs, both physical and spiritual. Are we emulating our Lord and Savior by showing philia love to all we encounter, or just to those whom we feel the love will be reciprocated?

Are we giving to the poor because we love them, or are we reverencing those who have riches in hopes they will give us some of their substances? Anapol (2011), argues that love is essentially free and cannot be bought, sold, traded, and by no means can anyone make another love them regardless of their peaked monetary status.   Are we comforting our brothers and sisters that need to be comforted? Jesus stated in Matthew 5:4-5, "Blessed are they that mourn: for they shall be comforted."   Are we visiting the sick and shut in or are we sending texts, cards, or virtually telling them I will pray for you (while many are drifting away in nursing homes)?   For heaven's sake, go and visit the brethren.   While praying is very significant and good, we also must show love in deeds.   James 5:13-15 (ESV) states, "Is anyone among you suffering?   Let him pray. Is anyone cheerful? Let him sing praise. Is anyone among you sick? Let him call for the elders of the church, and let them pray over him, anointing him with oil in the name of the Lord. And the prayer of faith will save the one who is sick, and the Lord will raise him up. And if he has committed sin, he will be forgiven."

What happened to philia love we once rendered toward one another?   Many of our brothers and sisters are homeless, hungry, and are in need of clothing.   Are we feeding the hungry and clothing the naked, or are we filling our own bellies (gluttonous) and building up our wardrobes to make a statement to the world?   Ezekiel 34:3-4 (ESV) reminds us, "You eat the fat, you clothe yourselves with the wool, you slaughter the fat ones, but you do not feed the sheep. The weak you have not strengthened, the sick you have not healed, the injured you have not bound up, the strayed you have not brought back, the lost you have not sought, and with force and harshness you have ruled them."

Have we turned back to our unrighteous ways? Jesus instructed us in Luke 3:11, "He that hath two coats, let him impart to him that hath none; and he that hath meat, let him do likewise." Let us feed our brethren with the Word of God, as well as nutritional foods, for who will listen if they are suffering from hunger pains? Let us feed our brothers and sisters who are hungry in our church homes before we reach out to those hungry in other cities, states, and countries. Yes, it is our Christian duty to take care of our brothers and sisters in our church family before we can care for others. Hunger has always been a major issue all over the world even America. In 2014, numerous Americans lived in households with insufficient food (48.1 million Americans; 32.8 million adults and 15.3 million children). In 2013 millions of seniors in America (5.4 million age 60 and over; or 9% of all seniors) lived in households with insufficient food (Feeding America, 2015). Not only are our brethren hungry for food and the Word of God, but they are lonely for fellowship while in nursing homes or incarcerated.

Is it not our duty as Christians to visit and assist our brother and sisters in nursing homes and prisons? What about the lost (individuals who do not know Jesus), are we telling them about our Lord and Savior Jesus Christ and that salvation is still free? Are we offering the lost, our neighbors, and our brethrens in Christ transportation to church and other places they may need to go, or are we too busy tending to our own needs? When was the last time we invited someone to come to Jesus, or merely to visit our church? Has going to church become a foolish formality without a desire to worship God? Do we desire to win souls for the Lord or just save ourselves? Let us refrain from being foolish as we were when we were in the world, for "the fool hath said in his heart there is no God" (Psalm 14:1).

Titus 3:3-5 (ESV) reminds us, "For we ourselves were once foolish, disobedient, led astray, slaves to various passions and pleasures, passing our days in malice and envy, hated by others and hating one another. But when the goodness and loving kindness of God our Savior appeared, he saved us, not because of works done by us in righteousness, but according to his own mercy, by the washing of regeneration and renewal of the Holy Spirit." Have we forgotten that we are representatives of Jesus Christ on a mission of winning souls for the building up of the body of Christ, or have we as Christians gone astray, back to our old sinful selfish ways?

What happened to the philia love we once showed for each other in the old days? I recall as a child how my parents freely provided for neighbors when they were low in substances (and vice versa). Frequently my parents would pick people up for church and take them to various places they needed to go. In fact, most neighbors on the block pitched in when someone was in need. We as Christians should be the main individuals to assist our brothers and sisters in need with a humble spirit. Paul in Romans 12:13 remind us of our duty to our brothers and sisters in Christ in stating, "Distributing to the necessity of saints; given to hospitality." Yet we as Christians are not assisting our brethren in Christ, let alone our neighbors.

Little to no Agape or philia love is emulated in our churches or the world. We as Christians and a nation must repent of our wrongful doings and turn back to God. *Lord thank you for your Grace and mercy in allowing us to repent; for we know if we do not repent, we will be destroyed. Strengthen us Father that we may become strong ambassadors in representing you and empower us with your Agape love to spread to one another, in Jesus Name, thank you.* As Ambassadors of Christ, we are to spread love and the good news of our Lord and Savior and what He has done for us, not malice.

"Let the redeemed of the LORD say so, whom he hath redeemed from the hand of the enemy" (Psalms 107:2), "For he has anointed me to bring good news to the poor; he has sent me to bind up the brokenhearted, to proclaim liberty to the captives, and the opening of the prison to those who are bound; to proclaim the year of the Lord's favor, and the day of vengeance of our God; to comfort all who mourn" (Isaiah 61:1-2). We as Christians must go back to our First Love (Jesus Christ) and stand guard as His true ambassador's spreading the love of God. When our brothers and sisters in Christ or our neighbors are in need of anything, let us show them love by making ourselves available and to assist them with their needs to the best of our ability. For how can we say that God abides in us and we have the love of God in our hearts but will not assist our brothers and sisters in need when we have been blessed with much substance (1st John 3:17)?

If we as Christians do not exemplify love for our

brothers and sisters in Christ, how can we be an example to others of the world and win them over to our Lord and Savior? We are to exemplify the same love that Christ has for the church towards our brothers and sisters, without showing jealously, hatred, or envy; neither should we gossip, bicker, or tear them down. The world is very much aware of what is happening in our churches and for the most part; many do not want to be affiliated with our churches for these very reasons. The desensitization of feelings expressed in our churches display everything except love to our biological, as well as spiritual brothers and sisters. Have we become like the children of Israel in our disobedience to God and have turned back to our wicked sinful ways? No storge, philia, or Agape love is being exemplified, just rebellion against God. *Restore us Lord!*

Isaiah 1:1-5 (ESV) relates to our rebellious nature just as the Israelites stating "The vision of Isaiah the son of Amoz, which he saw concerning Judah and Jerusalem in the days of Uzziah, Jotham, Ahaz, and Hezekiah, kings of Judah. - Hear, O heavens, and give ear, O earth; for the Lord has spoken: Children have I reared and brought up, but they have rebelled against me. The ox knows its owner, and the donkey its master's crib, but Israel does not know, my people do not understand. Ah, sinful nation, a people laden with iniquity, offspring of evildoers, children who deal corruptly! They have forsaken the Lord, they have despised the Holy One of Israel, they are utterly estranged. Why will you still be struck down? Why will you continue to rebel? The whole head is sick, and the whole heart faint."

Just as Israel, society as a whole epitomizes sin-sick souls, desensitized to storge, philia, and most importantly Agape Love. We must return to our First love (God) for healing. God is the only one who can instill Agape love in us. There is power in Agape *love* which causes one to love God, self, and others. Agape love binds and keeps us together (unity) while drawing others to God, which is the sole purpose of our existence, winning souls for the Lord and building up the body of Christ. We as a society coming together in fervent prayer will keep us bonded together; for prayer is significant in the eye of God and avails much. Yet, we must remain righteous as we bow down to our Father in prayer; let us continue to pray for forgiveness of our sins.

"For all have sinned, and come short of the glory of God; Being justified freely by his grace through the redemption that is in Christ Jesus: Whom God hath set forth to be a propitiation through faith in his blood, to declare his righteousness for the remission of sins that are past, through the forbearance of God; To declare, I say, at this time his righteousness: that he might be just, and the justifier of him which believeth in Jesus" (Romans 3:23-26). From the beginning of time, because of our fleshly sinful nature we have fallen short of the glory of God resulting in a set number of our earthly life. God states in Genesis 6:3 (ESV), "My Spirit shall not abide in man forever, for he is flesh: his days shall be 120 years." Psalm 90:10 states "The days of our years are threescore years and ten; and if by reason of strength they be fourscore years, yet is their strength labour and sorrow; for it is soon cut off, and we fly away." The word score is an old word for the number 20 (Wikipedia, 2014), therefore threescore years and ten equals 70, while fourscore years equal 80.

Regardless to the length of time God allows one to live on this earth, it is a blessing and should be valued and well utilize. Jesus earthly life (while short lived) was miraculous and well defined. Let us live exemplifying Jesus in our lives, for greater is our reward in heaven which is eternal life. Living a life emulating Jesus shows we love God while edifying others. As Christians, we must always reverence God and remember we are not our own, for we were brought with a price by Jesus Christ (1st Corinthians 7:23) who is the True vine, His Father God, is the husbandman, and we ourselves are the branches (John 15:1-2). Only in God do we live, move, and have our beings (Acts 17:28), for we all know that no branch can survive without the vine. Let us remain connected to the Vine. Jesus loves us, continues to forgive us, and wants us to remain connected to Him and one another.

Let us keep God first, for He will never leave or forsake us. Jesus is eternal and we will always need Him, in particular while living on this earth. Let us follow His commandments and love one another as He has loved us, for we all need each other. As a soloist (while ministering through song) I find one particular song comforting in discerning the significance of brotherly love. This song was written by David Frazier and composed by Bishop Hezekiah Walker, and titled; *I need you to survive*. The word *survival* best sums up the legacy of the Grammy-award winning Bishop Walker. After overcoming a tough childhood on the rough streets of Brooklyn, New York, and enduring the death of his father at the age of 14 (his mother passed away seven years later), God blessed him to surpass an environment overwhelmed with the majority of young men being destined for jail, drug addictions or an early grave (Cobb, 2005; New York Call, 2013).

Walker recalls the importance of being raised and immersed in the church which shielded him from his environment, and how going to church, listening to the music, and singing in the choir since the age of eight formed a sense of relief and increased his faith (New York Call, 2013). Below is a synopsis of the song, *I need you to Survive*:

I need you, you need me, we're all a part of God's body.

Stand with me; agree with me, we're all a part of God's body.

It is his will, that every need be supplied,
You are important to me, I need you to survive.
I pray for you; you pray for me, I love you, I need you to survive.
I won't harm you with words from my mouth,
I love you, I need you to survive.
It is his will, that every need be supplied.
You are important to me, I need you to survive.

While we may not be able to save everyone we certainly can love, help, and assist someone. Just as Bishop Hezekiah Walker found the church to be a refuge in his youth, the church and the elders in the church played an integral role in my childhood. Let us continue to look to our elders in our churches for guidance and prayer. Certainly, our elders have a great responsibility in demonstrating Agape love towards all even when one shows hatred toward them; for they are God's anointed servants on earth, leading the way. Almighty God "gave the apostles, the prophets, the evangelists, the shepherds and teachers to equip the saints for the work of ministry, for building up the body of Christ" (Ephesians 4:11-12, ESV). Are we carrying out our duties as saints of God in showing love for one another? God sees and hears all and He knows if we are rendering Agape love toward our brothers, sisters, and neighbors. We as Christians have a responsibility to be more loving, caring, and assist our brothers and sisters to come to Jesus. We must love from our hearts, "For the life of grace in the heart of a regenerate person, is the beginning and first principle of a life of glory, whereof they must be destitute who hate their brother in their hearts" (Henry, 2014). Christians are the stronger vessels and must build up the weaker individuals; not tear them down? Paul in Romans 15:1-7 (NIV) states:

> We who are strong ought to bear with the failings of the weak and not to please ourselves. Each of us should please our neighbors and continue to build them up. For even Christ did not please himself but, as it is written: The insults of those who insult you have fallen on me. For everything that was written in the past was written to teach us, so that through the endurance taught in the scriptures and the

encouragement they provide we might have hope. May the God who gives endurance and encouragement give you the same attitude of mind toward each other that Christ Jesus had, so that with one mind and one voice you may glorify the God and Father of our Lord Jesus Christ. Accept one another, then, just as Christ accepted you, in order to bring praise to God (p.1).

We as Christians must work together in unity, "with all humility and gentleness, with patience, bearing with one another in love, eager to maintain the unity of the Spirit in the bond of peace" (Ephesians 4:2-3, ESV). For we do not want to leave this earth and face rejection while trying to enter into Heaven (thinking we did all what we were commissioned to do). Again the question is asked, are we exhibiting Agape love, or are we as Christian's mimicking the world or the Pharisees? For we know that everyone who calls on the Lord will not enter into Heaven, only those who are obedient to the Word of God will enter in. *Have mercy Lord*; and when judgment day comes, many will say to the Lord, how in His name they worked many miracles, but because they were not obedient and faithful in showing true love toward one another in particular, those in need; God will tell them to depart from Him for He know them not (Matthew 6:21-23).

There is no quid-pro-quo (trade off) in Jesus Christ. God wants us to come to Him freely, and in doing so, we as Christians must love everyone and treat all the same way we want to be treated (Luke 6:31).

Certainly life can challenge us as a boomerang; we should always treat people kindly, for one never knows if they may need assistance in the future. While we may have good health and doing financially well today, we do not know what the next hour, minute, or second holds for us. As quoted by Graves (n.d.), "I don't know what the future holds for me, but I know who holds the future" even if it's a testing of our faith. Furthermore, we do not want to miss the mark of entering into the Kingdom of Heaven which is our ultimate goal. Matthew 25:44-45 confirms that many will miss the mark in his recording, "Then shall they also answer him, saying, Lord, when saw we thee a hungred, or athirst, or a stranger, or naked, or sick, or in prison, and did not minister unto thee? Then shall he answer them, saying, verily I say unto you, inasmuch as ye did it not to one of the least of these, ye did it not to me." Let us treat everyone with respect and love regardless of their outer appearance or status.

Yes, many of us are guilty (intentionally and unintentionally) of making judgments on individuals that are less fortunate (poor or homeless) than ourselves and may even criticize them, and make negative connotations concerning their lifestyles and how their lives would be better if they found Jesus. Yet we forget that everyone was not meant to be well off or rich. STOPPED The Word of God tells us "For the poor shall never cease out of the land: therefore I command thee, saying, Thou shalt open thine hand wide unto thy brother, to thy poor, and to thy needy, in thy land" (Deuteronomy 15:11). As representatives of Christ we are to assist anyone we encounter in need regardless of their status. As Dr. Martin Luther King Jr. profoundly quoted, "Life's most persistent and urgent question is, what are you doing for others?" (Brainy Quote, 2015). Oh how precious is the Word of God in providing scriptures, parables, and examples to assist all who thirst for righteousness, love, and the truth. We must not only read the Word of God, but live by the Word of God.

Living by Example

Two women in the Bible that exhibited Philia love (in my honest opinion) were Ruth and Lydia. The story of Ruth is threefold in delivering a message: first in denoting ramifications of individuals and nations when they are disobedient to God's statures (Judges, Naomi's sons marrying forbidden women), second in demonstrating philia love, faithfulness, and patience in which God wants us to show towards one another, and third in showing how God can and will deliver, save, and bless anyone who are obedient to His statures (Ruth, Naomi). Ruth exemplified great philia love for her mother-in-law Naomi during her time of distress. Let's recall the story of Ruth as foretold in the history section of the Old Testament of the Holy Bible. A man by the name of Elimelech, his wife Naomi, and their two sons Mahlon and Chilion (Israelites) lived in Bethlehem during the time of the Judges. A famine developed in the land and they moved to a nearby country called Moab. Naomi's husband Elimelech died and her sons went against God's ordinances (Deuteronomy 23: 3) and married Moabite women; Mahlon married Ruth and Chilion married Orpah.

Unfortunately, years later Naomi's sons also died leaving her with two daughter-in-laws. Naomi decides to return to Bethlehem without her daughter-in-laws; however, one daughter-in-law (Ruth) refuses to leave Naomi's side and chooses to serve Naomi's God (Ruth 1:16). After returning to Bethlehem Naomi's relative Boaz (well-off) shows favor to Ruth and allows her to glean in his fields while informing his workers to purposely leave extra grain for her. Naomi in recognizing Boaz's favor toward Ruth instructs her to seek marriage with Boaz as a kinsman redeemer. Ruth in being obedient to Naomi does as instructed and Boaz agrees after seeking proper ordinances. The offspring of Boaz and Ruth marriage was a son named Obed, the grandfather of King David, in the lineage of our Savior Jesus Christ our Messiah. What a great example of storge, philia, and Agape love.

Lydia is another woman mentioned in the Bible who demonstrated philia love. Lydia was an Asiatic, and her native city was Thyatria where Jehovah was worshipped by a strong Jewish element, however the chief object of worship was Apollo (worshiped as the sun-god under the name of Tyrinnus). Thyatira was known for its many guilds and one being that of *dyers* (Lockyer, 2011). The water was well-adapted for dyeing and producing unique permanent scarlet cloth in which no other place could compare which made the city well renowned and productive. Lydia was one of the main sellers of this product (Acts 16:14) resulting in her wealth and success in the business sector (Lockyer, 2011). As a prosperous business woman Lydia hired servants to attend to her needs in her *owned* spacious home.

Lydia although not a Christian and in spite of her busy obligations to her business made time to worship God by attending daily prayer meetings held at the riverside (Lockyer, 2011). After hearing the teaching of Christ through Apostle Paul Lydia's faith strengthened (Psalm 119:18, 130; Luke 24:45), she received Christ as her Savior, became Paul's first European convert, and was baptized. Lydia in sharing this information with her household staff caused them also to become baptized believers serving God (Lockyer, 2011). Lydia used a great deal of her profits from her business to assist God's servants in the work of the Gospel, while showing them affection and hospitality in her home.

Lydia showed kindness to all she encountered, won souls for the Lord, exhibited love through hospitality, and boldly took care of Paul and Silas (beaten and worn out) in her home (Lockyer, 2011) after their release from prison (1st Timothy 5:10; Hebrews 13:2; 1 Peter 4:9). Paul highly appreciated Lydia kindness and hospitality and upon writing his letter to the Philippians he included Lydia to the saints at Philippi to whom he sent his salutations (Philippians 1:1-7). Paul also recognized Lydia as one of the women who labored with him in the Gospel (Philippians 4:3) and she certainly showed love through her actions as noted in (Romans 12:11), "Not slothful in business, fervent in spirit, serving the Lord." Lydia showed loved and reverence for God by not letting her secular prosperous business interfere with her daily submission and service to the Lord (Lockyer, 2011).

Lydia in obedience to God showed loved for her sisters and brothers in Christ by showing them hospitality in her home, feeding, and caring for them when needed (Lockyer, 2011). All can learn from these examples of philia love displayed by Lydia. Anapol (2011) derived an excellent definition of true love in stating, "Love cares what becomes of you because love knows that we are all interconnected. Love is inherently compassionate and empathic. Love knows that the "other" is also oneself. This is the true nature of love and love itself cannot be manipulated or restrained. Love honors the sovereignty of each soul. Love is its' own law" (p.1). While many are aware of Agape love as demonstrated by our Lord and Savior Jesus Christ, still many continue to work contrary in spreading false love in various ways that lacks Godly morals, values, and statures. This fallacy love that is emerging daily nationwide instead of Agape Love is Eros love.

CHAPTER 4
THY BED DEFILED OR UNDEFILED?

Eros Love

Eros in Greek (ηρως) religion is intimate love and relates to the god of love and his Roman equal who name was Cupid meaning desire (Encyclopaedia Britannica, 2013). Be not mistaken, Eros love is admirable when a couple is married as epitomized when God made Adam and Eve (Genesis 3:20) and united them in holy matrimony. In Genesis 1: 28 God approved Adam and Eve's marriage and blessed them and instructed them to ". . . Be fruitful, and multiply, and replenish the earth, and subdue it . . ." In addition, Hebrews 13: 4 proclaims, "Marriage is honorable in all, and the bed undefiled: but whoremongers and adulterers God will judge." While many Christians and non-Christians attempt to follow this command many fail in remaining obedient to this ordinance due to our sinful nature in lusting of the flesh. Without a doubt, societal mass media (television, DVD movies, internet, etc.,) assist highly in enticing individuals to have sex outside of marriage in promotion of Eros love as the new era; *It's your thing do what you want to do.* Still, having sex outside of marriage is a sin in the eyesight of God. We must stay in prayer to our Heavenly Father for strength in this area instead of making excuses.

Strengthening the Flesh

Many in giving in to the flesh try to justify their sinful acts in employing scripture spoken by Jesus in Matthew 26:40 while speaking to his disciples, "The spirit is willing, but the flesh is weak." *Help us Lord!* Nonetheless, Galatians 6:8 contends, "For he that soweth to his flesh shall of the flesh reap corruption; but he that soweth to the Spirit shall of the Spirit reap life everlasting." Still, many (Christians and non-Christians) choose to remain single while fulfilling the lust of the flesh. 1st John 2:16 reminds us that, For all that is in the world, the lust of the flesh, and the lust of the eyes . . . is not of the Father, but is of the world. Galatians 5: 16-17 reminds us to ". . . Walk in the spirit, and ye shall not fulfil lust of the flesh, For the flesh lusteth against the Spirit, and the spirit against the flesh." In agreement with the Word of God, Eros love is commissioned for marriage, "Wives, submit yourselves unto your own husbands, as unto the Lord" (Ephesians 5: 22). Let us stay in fervent prayer and not cling to the activities of this world that are merely the acts of the enemy in deceiving all that can be deceived, for there are ramifications for disobeying God's ordinances as displayed in the Word of God.

Beware of Deceivers

The Bible speaks of two women who truly demonstrated defiled Eros love, one being Jezebel and the other being Delilah. Jezebel (worshiper of Baal; violation of the 1st Commandment of God, Mark 12: 29) although beautiful to the eye was devious and powerful. Queen Jezebel was the daughter of the past King of Sidon (Eth-baal) who also worshipped Baal and was a murderer (1st Kings 16:31), she was married to King Ahab (one could argue she was in charge) in Israel and she sought and had many of God's prophets killed. Jezebel was known for her idolatry, whoredom, witchcraft, murdering (shedding of innocent blood), cruelty, and persecution of God's prophets (1st Kings 18: 4). Jezebel not only persecuted many of God's prophets, but she taught and led God's bond servants of Thyatira into committing acts of immorality and eating meats sacrificed to idols as the Balaamites and Nicolaitans (Revelations 2:6, 14, 15). In Revelations 2: 20, God speaks to the Pastor of church in Thyatira through the revelation (disclosure) of His beloved Apostle John while he was a prisoner in Rome (imprisoned for preaching the Word of Jesus Christ) on an isolated desert in Patmos (Skolfield, n.d.).

John informed the leader of the church how God recognized their previous love, faith, service, and perseverance in their service but rebuked him for the present acts of allowing Jezebel to lead them astray (Revelations 2:20). Jezebel being egotistical showed no respect or love for the *One and Only True God.* Apparently, the knowledge of God's love was ignorant for her, for God's love is not self seeking (1st Corinthians 13:5). Jezebel's last threat was to kill one of God's major Prophets (Elijah; the only prophet courageous to stand against her) and his devotees (1 Kings 16:29-34;

18:17-40; 19:1-3; 21:1-16; 22:29-40; 2 Kings 9:21-28; 9:30-37).

Favorably, Jezebel did not succeed in killing Elijah but was killed herself when Jehu (captain of Israel's Northern Kingdom army) ordered several of Jezebel's eunuchs to throw her out of the palace window. Jezebel's blood splattered the wall and her body was trampled by horses. Later, Jehu ordered her body to be buried; however dogs had eaten her flesh and the only remains were her skull, feet, and hands (2nd Kings 9: 32-36). Strangely, prior to Jehu's arrival Jezebel had put on eye make-up, fixed her hair, and looked out of the window. While one theorist contend Jezebel's aim was to seduce Jehu (Bromiley, 1995), a different theorist argued she was adorning herself for burial as a queen (Asimov, 1988). *Defiled Eros love has its ramifications.*

Another woman in the Bible who displayed defiled Eros love was Delilah (believed to be a harlot and Philistine; Exum, 2015) who spearheaded the downfall of Samson the strongest man in the Bible to ever live. Samson was a Nazirite dedicated to God from his mother's womb and was to never cut his seven locks of hair in which his strength resided (Judges 16:13). While Samson knew God, he loved Philistine women and had recently lain with a Philistine prostitute (Judges 16: 1-3). Samson led Israel for 20 years fighting against the Philistines (Judges 16:31).

Yet, Samson was betrayed by Delilah (his lover) after revealing to her where his strength originated. Delilah was persistent in nagging and pasturing Samson to reveal where his strength came from. Three times she was unsuccessful in gaining the truth but the fourth try Samson informed her. Samson loved Delilah, but Delilah loved money. She was promised 1,100 pieces of silver *from each* Philistine ruler (Judges 16:5). There were five rulers representing the five important Philistine city-states (Exum, 2015; Judges 3:3), resulting in a total of 5,500 pieces of silver Delilah was to receive. According to one scholar, the American dollar amount of this betrayal was $89, 641 (Stewart, 2012).   The aftermath of this betrayal caused Samson's eyes to be gouged out, head shaven bald and his captivity by the Philistines' his enemies (Judges 16:4-20).

After being captured and made to entertain the Philistines Sampson's hair begin to grow back. Samson despised the Philistines who believed that their god was responsible for his capture. Upon being led by a servant to entertain the Philistines Samson asked to be guided between the two pillars that held up the temple so that he could lean against them. Samson then prayed to God for the return of his strength to destroy the Philistines for taking his eyesight and to die along with them. God answered Samson's prayers and about three thousand men and women were destroyed (this included all the rulers of the Philistines) along with Samson. The bodily remains of Samson was recovered by his family and buried in the tomb of his father (Judges 16: 23-31).   Defiled Eros love (sexual immorality) is a sin in the sight of God (2nd Corinthians 12: 21).

In fact, worldwide exploiting of defiled Eros love over social media in my humble opinion is the work of the deceiver.   Let us not be deceived and remain focused on God who is the only one that can shield us from the fiery darts of Satan. Man can be deceived but not God, let us continue to trust Him who has our best interest at heart and will keep us from being led into temptations such as defiled Eros love. For "God is not a man, that he should lie; neither the son of man, that he should repent: hath he said, and shall he not do it? Or hath he spoken, and shall he not make it good?" (Numbers 23: 19).

Nationwide many are seeking and indulging in defiled Eros love versus philia and Agape. The enemy's time is running out so he is deceiving as many as possible by any means necessary. The Word of God forewarned us that in the last days men will become lovers of themselves; we are now living in perilous times. Confirmation: "But mark this: There will be terrible times in the last days. People will be lovers of themselves, lovers of money, boastful, proud, abusive, disobedient to their parents, ungrateful, unholy, without love, unforgiving, slanderous, without self-control, brutal, not lovers of the good, treacherous, rash, conceited, lovers of pleasure rather than lovers of God, having a form of godliness but denying its power. Have nothing to do with such people (2nd Timothy 3:1-5, NIV).

Yet many are content with what the world has to offer in relationship to defiled Eros love and daily log into chat rooms (Craigslist, Facebook, etc.) via the internet and other electronic devices. While many are deceived (some to the extent of death) others continue to use them and arrange to meet unknown individuals. Since 1995, over 400 homicides have been linked to online dating (Wikipedia, 2015a), and as to Facebook, police report every 40 minutes a crime is linked to facebook. In 2012, officers logged 12, 300 alleged offences and investigations referencing murder, rape, child sex offences, assault, kidnap, death threats, witness intimidation, and fraud, all linked to Facebook the popular social networking site (Doyle, 2012). But still there is hope for our nation if we return to our Father who loves us and is waiting to forgive us. God longs to release the shackles we have sustained from this world, for there is power in the Name of Jesus and He can break all chains, for it is the *Power of Agape Love!* Nonetheless, what is Agape Love?

CHAPTER 5
POWER IN THE NAME

Agape Love

The origin of the word Agape first appeared in 1607, Late Latin, from Greek (αγάπη), meaning love. Agape is unconditional love, the love God has for humans (Merriam-Webster, 2013). Laurie (2015) defines Agape love as intense, complete, devoted, sacrificial love. Agape love appears to be challenging for all and incorporates holistic (spiritual, physical, emotional, and psychological) affection. Agape is the greatest love illustrated by God in giving the world His son Jesus Christ to die on the cross for the remission of our sins. Jesus stated in John 3: 16, "For God so loved the world that He gave His only Begotten Son, that whosoever believeth in Him should not perish, but have everlasting life."

Agape love causes Christians to surrender to Jesus Christ as their Savior and depart from all other gods. For Jesus loves and cares for us and are concerned where we will spend eternity. Only through Him can we be changed from our sinful nature to a Godly persona. When we accept Jesus Christ as our Lord and Savor God begins a work in us that empowers us to change and please Him; therefore we no longer are indulged in pleasing ourselves, but the love of God causes us to please Him and others. Surely, we may fall short but God gives us an inner spirit which convicts us when we do things that are not pleasing in His sight; and because of the nature of His love, when we confess our sins, He forgives and embraces us back into the fold and uses us to accomplish His will. Philippians 2:13 confirms that "For it is God which worketh in you both to will and to do of his good pleasure."

We must put God first in all of our endeavors, for He is worthy. Jesus stated in Matthew 6:24-25, "No man can serve two masters: for either he will hate the one, and love the other; or else he will hold to the one, and despise the other. Ye cannot serve God and mammon. Therefore I say unto you, take no thought for your life, what ye shall eat, or what ye shall drink; nor yet for your body, what ye shall put on. Is not the life more than meat, and the body than raiment?"

No, we cannot serve two masters, through Jesus we become slaves of righteousness. "Do you not know that if you present yourselves to anyone as obedient slaves, you are slaves of the one whom you obey, either of sin, which leads to death, or of obedience, which leads to righteousness? But thanks be to God, that you who were once slaves of sin have become obedient from the heart to the standard of teaching to which you were committed, and, having been set free from sin, have become slaves of righteousness" (Romans 6: 16-18, ESV).

For only Jesus is worthy to be forefront and praised, "Surely he hath borne our griefs, and carried our sorrows: yet we did esteem him stricken, smitten of God, and afflicted. But he was wounded for our transgressions; he was bruised for our iniquities: the chastisement of our peace was upon him; and with his stripes we are healed" (Isaiah 53:4-5). Jesus states in John 13: 34, "A new commandment I give unto you, that ye love one another; as I have loved you, that ye also love one another." Agape love is so powerful that God finds glory when one loves those that do not love them.

Yes, loving someone when they do not love you is very challenging for Christians as well as non-Christians. Yet, we as Christians must love everyone including our enemies; *this is powerful!* Jesus states in Matthew 5:43-48, "You have heard that it was said, You shall love your neighbor and hate your enemy. But I say to you, love your enemies and pray for those who persecute you, so that you may be sons of your Father who is in heaven. For he makes his sun rise on the evil and on the good and sends rain on the just and on the unjust. For if you love those who love you, what reward do you have? Do not even the tax collectors do the same? And if you greet only your brothers, what more are you doing than others? Do not even the Gentiles do the same? You therefore must be perfect, as your heavenly Father is perfect." *Love is so potent.*

Dr. Martin Luther King Jr. argued, "Love is the only force capable of transforming an enemy to a friend" (Goodreads, 2014). According to Lamb (2015), "Agape love is sacrificial, selfless, pure, unconditional, holy, honoring, and out of this world, it's the love Jesus has for us, and tells us to have for others" (pg. 1). Agape love keeps one from cherishing the flesh and respect the liberty God has given us and allow us to serve each other in love (Galatians 5:13). As Paul articulates in this passage under the New Covenant, we were given freedom to love our neighbors as ourselves in a spiritual way not to participate in sinful ways. Agape Love instills in us humility, gentleness, patience, and causes us to bear with each other in love (Ephesians 4:2) this keeps us in the Spirit of unity and harmony.

Surely, there will be times that individuals will challenge our intellect and may even provoke us to anger; these are the times that we must fall on our knees and ask God for strength. God's Word reminds us in 1st Peter 5:7, to cast all of our anxieties on the Lord for He cares for us, for when you cry unto the Lord, He will help you (Psalms 30:2) and heal your wounded spirit (Jeremiah 30:17; Psalms 147: 3). No matter what the cost, we as Christians must demonstrate Agape Love in representation of Our Lord and Savor Jesus Christ. Agape Love is the unsurpassed love Jesus has for us (the Church) as stated in Matthew 16:18, ". . . upon this rock I will build my church; and the gates of hell shall not prevail against it." Incidentally, the word church; ekklesia, is a Greek word (ecclesia;Latin) meaning a called out (Cooper, n.d.).

Christ loved the church so greatly that He gave himself for it, "That he might sanctify and cleanse it with the washing of water by the Word, that he might present it to himself a glorious church, not having spot, or wrinkle, or any such thing; but that it should be holy and without blemish" (Ephesians 5: 25-27). How powerful is this that we as the church (His bride) are so loved by Jesus Christ (The Bridegroom) in spite of our sinful nature. Howbeit, we sin over and over yet; God forgives us because of His Nature and Agape Love. When we accept Jesus as our Lord and Savor His Grace flourishes us and He clothes us in His righteousness. What greater Love can anyone give?

In Revelations chapters 2-3, Jesus speaks to the angels of the seven churches (*Ephesus*; the loveless church, *Smyrna*; the persecuted church, *Pergamum*; the compromising church, *Thyatira*; the corrupt church, *Sardis*; the dead church, *Philadelphia*; the faithful church, and *Laodicea*; the lukewarm church) which were all located in Asia minor within a 90 mile radius of each other; distance being 25 to 50 miles between them (Valdez, 2014). Although Christ loves the church (representing the Body of Christ), He is not pleased when we do not reverence Him, showing little to no enthusiasm in praising Him, and show a declination in our zeal, patience, humbleness, and seriousness, toward Him.

When we as Christian becomes slothful in our services to God and ultimately slip back into our sinful ways, we will face consequences. For God is worthy of great praise, and we should praise Him always. Still, because of His Agape love God warns us, chastises us, and gives us recurring chances to repent of our sins and return whole heartily to Him. Jesus stated in Revelations 3: 19-22:

> As many as I love, I rebuke and chasten: be
> zealous therefore, and repent. Behold, I stand

at the door, and knock: if any man hear my voice, and open the door, I will come in to him, and will sup with him, and he with me. To him that overcometh will I grant to sit with me in my throne, even as I also overcame, and am set down with my Father in his throne. He that hath an ear, let him hear what the Spirit saith unto the churches.

We the church (the called –out) in particular must pray without ceasing (1st Thessalonians 5:17) while asking for forgiveness, for we are representatives of our Lord and savior Jesus Christ and must imitate Him in all our endeavors. We must continue to spread Agape love even when love is not reciprocated, we must love one another for this is God's supreme commandment.

The Greatest Commandments

Our Lord and Savior in a public discussion with the Scribes, Pharisees, and Sadducees stated the greatest commandments concerning love. Jesus stated, ". . . The first of all the commandments are, Hear, O Israel; The Lord our God is one Lord: And thou shalt love the Lord thy God with all thy heart, and with all thy soul, and with all thy mind, and with all thy strength: this is the first commandment. And the second is like, namely this, Thou shalt love thy neighbour as thyself. There is none other commandment greater than these" (Mark 12: 29-31). One could question, who is our neighbor and what does *love* have to do with anything in today's' society?

Jesus describes in a parable (short story used to show a moral or spiritual lesson) a neighbor as being anyone in need and a good neighbor as one who has mercy on the one in need (Luke 10: 29-37). Amazing, how this parable does not exempt anyone: mother, father, sister, brother, children, friends, and non-friends. For no one knows (rich or poor) if they will ever be in need. As Christians, we should be forerunners in demonstrating love and compassion for one another, but as in the parable concerning a man in dire need, the priest and Levite passed him by while a stranger (called a good Samaritan) stopped and took care of him. For clarity; many Levites were known to be priest however, some were not priests, but assigned duties in the tabernacles (Numbers 3-4) to assist the priests (Numbers 1:50; 3:6, 8; 16:9; 1 Chronicles 9:22). This parable spoken by Jesus confirms that love has everything to do with the viability of society and most importantly entering into the kingdom of Heaven.

As Christians, God instructs us to love everyone and let our light ". . . shine before men, that they may see your good works and glorify your Father in heaven" (Matthew 5:16). Christians demonstrating love toward one another reflects the love embedded in us from God and may ultimately cause non-Christians to follow Christ. As Christians are we truly displaying Jesus in our lives, not only on Sundays but in our daily walk? Or have we lost the true meaning of love and fellowship, and are now following worldly practices? Has society influenced our hearts and caused us to become waxed cold in relationship to loving others? Are we spending more hours reading, studying, and reflecting on God's Word versus watching television, playing video games, and tweeting our peers on social media? Often times, we are unaware of the great influences the media plays on us.

Has our focus on Christ deviated (dimming our lights) leading us back into darkness (worldly ways)? Apostle Paul in Ephesians 5:8 while using an analogy of family and church states, "For we were sometimes darkness, but now are ye light in the Lord: walk as children of light." Have we, the called-out lost our love and faith in God and are willing to defend the change? Have we lost our Christian values, faith, and our position in God by becoming materialistic worshippers?

Pastor Jake Gaines (2015) questions, "Why do many Christians endure painstaking efforts to defend and protect material things but put so little effort into defending their faith? The answer is painfully simple, it's not valuable enough" (p. 15). *Amen* . . . Pastor Gaines goes on to say that we as Christians have an amazing position as a Christian called *My Spot* which is secured by the blood of Jesus. In this particular position, it is our responsibility to live it out to the glory of God. When we accepted Jesus as our Lord and Savior we denounced society, our way, our purposes, and our methods; simply put, we decided to follow Jesus and become Christ-like. Perhaps, our first love has become electronic devices instead of Jesus.

Agape Love versus Electronic Love

What happened to our values in relationship to the love we as Christians once expressed toward one another, regardless of their faults? As a society, we are living in times in which liberty is greatly exemplified in the retention of education, homes, cars, and even our finances (to the extent of investing in stock), yet we have become loveless and desensitized to our fellowman. This simply is not Agape love but selfishness and we still are not satisfied and full of worries. While living in times of uncertainty we find ourselves worrying constantly concerning mediocre things in which we really have little or no control over, instead of assurance (where will we spend eternity). Nevertheless, we say we love and have faith in God, but repeatedly seek other means to resolve our problems.

For the most part, some of us have left our First love and no longer depend on God, but cling to sources of the world via electronic devices to pacify us. While electronic devices grant us relevant/irrelevant accessibility to various resources, they also have potentials to cause alienation from God and subsequently cause us to be deceived by Satan. Have we as a society lost our connection with God and are now blindly in love with technology? Research shows that within the last 500 years technology has grown exponentially, and mass media has basically taken over many of our households replacing parents' love with technology and worldly love. While we once relied on truths from reading the Word of God, books, magazines, newspapers, listening to the radio, watching sensible television, we now solely rely on information retrieved from the worldwide web via our cellular phones and other electronic devices (Patel, 2015).

In fact, one may not admit it, but cellular phones have caused many to cease visiting family members and friends. Instead of telephone calls or home visits, these acts of love and kindness have been replaced with text messages and information imputed on social Medias. Are we coming together as a village with brotherly love as God instructed, or have our *village collapsed* due to the influences of the social media on the World Wide Web such as Blogs, Virtual Worlds, Facebook, Twitter, Instagram, YouTube, and others (too many to name)? Has this new era of social media changed or influenced our perspectives of love toward one another? While there is nothing wrong in developing new skills to keep up with the new era as in texting or blogging one another, we must not let this new era replace our traditional ways in visiting our love ones and friends.

Have we changed from stability in God to instability based upon information retrieved from mass media sites? Have we forgotten that God gives man knowledge to create new technology? Be not misguided new technologies are not appalling; it is how one employs the technology that can be devastating. Are we using any of our technical devices to glorify God? Impressive are various reputable sites (scholarly; peer reviewed, health, education, factual religion, etc) retrievable on the World Wide Web; but beware there are numerous non- reputable sites (pornography, Islamic State in Iraq and Syria (ISIS) beheadings, etc) that many use for vain reasons. One researcher study contends, "The Web has been criticized for elevating rumors to the level of news, making inappropriate material available to children, collecting private information about users, and creating a false sense of intimacy and interaction among users" (Hanson, 2015, p, 1). Researchers Paul, Singh, & Sunita (2013) assert:

In general, the mass media is a means to deliver information from a source of information (communicator) to the recipient information (communicants). The entry of information by the mass media impact social change in society. Information thus has the power both to *build* and *destroy*. This means that the mass media in this is double-faced. Information, that until society can be taken differently, by each individual depending on their interests, and depends on society's ability in using information coming proportionally. The most contrasting impact is felt among the community is changing lifestyles and patterns of behavior which society requires to be versatile instant, causing a shift of cultural values in public life. Mass media presence is felt more influence on the younger generation who are in the stage of self. The information received from the media is affecting the social and cultural life of a society both in the perception of his attitude and behavior. Mass media has created a new culture that wants the public to adjust to the culture. Adjustment of public attitudes toward popular culture caused a social change in all dimensions of public life and public demands for change from traditional society to the society with a modern lifestyle (p. 38).

While technology lends one worldwide fingertip access 24/7; many sites offer deceitful information causing some to be deceived and condemned. God offers one worldwide 24/7 access without a finger, without time delay, without a chance of information breaches, and without condemnation. In God we have liberty (2nd Corinthians 3:17) and no condemnation (Romans 8:1). While the world is quickly to condemn (righteous/unrighteous), God can give one eternal life in heaven. Employing technology in an appropriate manner is good; however, one must be careful when disseminating personal information on social media. We must be mindful that information communicated in e-mails and texts are always retrievable even when deleted. As with all technology, the employment of its usage is up to the individual, whether one employs the media for good/bad or exemplifies love/hate. Are we guilty of both?

For the most part, the love that we once stressed towards our family members and fellow man now comes thru social media (in particular Facebook), e-mails, or texts. Frequently one may miss a family or friend's scheduled event due to one not being registered on Facebook. *Help us Lord!* Upon missing and finding out about the past event, replies are simply, *I sent it on Facebook!* One can agree that in the past many of us called our love ones on the phone to invite them to special events, but how many of us still call, or send out mailed invitations to our love ones and friends? *Have Mercy Lord!* Thank God for His Agape Love in not having us reach Him by texts or emails, in Jesus' Name, Amen!

Heartbreaking; Agape love is not shown to our family members, let alone toward our friends. Yet, we say the love of God is in our hearts. Have we become our own gods? What happened to love thy neighbor as thyself? Have we become lovers of ourselves and our cell phones? We use to thank God for waking us up in the mornings, now we thank our cell phones (after setting the alarm). We use to check our answering machines for phones messages, now we check our cell phones. We use to verbally communicate with each other at home, work, etc., but now we employ our cell phones. We use to ponder our brains and critically think out situations or pray to God for resolutions, but now we rely on information retrieved from our cell phones or the internet.

One could argue that electronic devices have become our 1st love and no longer God. Sending cards and letters were authentic in nature as a touch of love, yet now we send e-mails or texts. We as a nation have become too impatient with each other, too relaxed in acceptance of wrongs, and too content with electronic devices. Still, we call this love, sending text verses visiting, calling on the telephone, writing a letter, or sending a card (sorry, electronic cards are not the same as hard copies). Why not stop by and show someone your love; for love is an action word! Merely asked, what happen to our pride, values, beliefs, and morals? Has our pride disintegrated since our decision-making and values are now based on social media data? Are we not aware that the social media influences have become so powerful that we may be reverencing them as our gods?

Even the television media (multiple channels) broadly exposes one to any and everything that is happening in the world (good or bad). Collectively, the television media greatly enlightens one concerning celebrities and their ungodly lifestyles, violence, immoral sexuality, and other vast subjects. Rarely, does one hear good or Godly news concerning celebrities or anyone else. Thank God for some spiritual inclined services shown on television; but watch it, we must still read the Word of God for ourselves. Yes, we have been forewarned concerning the many false prophets in the world (Matthews 7:15: 2nd Peter 2:1; 1st John 4:1). God forbid, one of the false prophets may be the forerunner for the antichrist and are on a mission of gaining and marking Satan worshippers. Speaking of markers, many believe the implanting of microchips in humans is the mark of the beast (Heaven Questions.com, 2015). If this happens, will we choose Agape love or electronic chip love?

Regrettably, we are living in a society that because of havoc, the installation of microchips appears to be the best new security method. Nevertheless; the implantation of these chips will leave our lives even more impersonal. Have we as a society condemned Agape love and feel more secure with electronic chips? Have we forgotten God is the Universe? Have we forgotten that God is Omnipotence, Omniscience, and Omnipresence? Agape loves allows us free will and when we accept Jesus Christ as our Savior and continue to be obedient to Him we will live with Him eternally after death. On the other hand, micro and biochips are meant to be impersonal and are highly traceable. While the installations of micro-chips in credit cards in attempt to limit fraudsters are welcoming, the implantations of these devices in humans for some individual are unwelcoming.

Many believe the implanting of these chips in humans is Satan's handy work and are employed to deceive users. Howbeit, the Food and Drug Administration have approved the implantation of the microchip for medical purposes. The microchip (size of a grain of rice) is cheap, quickly implanted (about 20 minutes), does not require sutures, sends out signals that identify individuals whereabouts every day, and the unique battery is constantly recharged (heat fluctuations) by the human body. In essence, the battery wears out when the person dies (Heaven Questions.com, 2015). The implanted biochip stores up to 15 digits (currently used to track pets) and when implanted can be scanned for one's personal identification number (PIN). Once scanned, a global centralized computer system can perform functions against your PIN number.

In addition, there are the existences of completely tamper-proof biometric identification technology devices that are greatly considered more reliable than the biochip in identifying or recognizing individuals by numbers as in eye-scans, fingerprints, hand scans, and voice identification (Watkins, 1999). Believe it or not, many individuals in our present society desire to be micro chipped, and very much welcome any and all electronic devices. Many voice the implantation of the microchip will solve a lot of the world's problems such as getting rid of criminals, perverts, protect one's identification, protect the elderly and children from harm, keeps one from having to carry cash and credit cards, and will end terrorism (Heaven Questions.com, 2015). *Have mercy Lord, help us!* How can one honestly believe a microchip will rid the world of undesirables? Only obedience to God will resolve our worldly problems, for God loves us and hold our best interest at heart. Why not accept Agape love, be obedient to His Word, and stay in prayer?

In the times-of-old our parents and forefathers leaned and depended on God, stayed in constant prayer, and showed Agape Love to one another. Nonetheless, we are living in a society that waivers Agape love until something drastically happens. We have stopped praying in our homes (even over our food), we have stopped kneeling down on our knees and praying to God in our churches, and for the most part, we did nothing to keep prayer in our schools. Yet we ask, what has happened to our world, there is so much hatred for one another instead of love? Are we praying to God to change our society?

Over 53 years ago (June 25, 1962) the U.S. Supreme Court removed prayer from our nation's schools and millions of our children were forbidden to publicly announce the name of our Lord and Savior at the beginning of each school day which ultimately led to a decline in our nation's morality (Bergel, 1988). The *Engel v. Vitale*, 370 U.S. 421 (1962), was a landmark United States Supreme Court case that ruled it is unconstitutional for state officials to compose an official school prayer and encourage its recitation in public schools. *Wrong verdict!* Amazing how a few individuals caused prayer to be removed from an entire nation public school system.

Recap: The Steven, I. Engel, et al. v. William J. Vitale, Jr., et al (State) case was initiated by the Engel family; a group of other families belonging to schools in New Hyde Park, New York supported the Engels in complaining that the voluntary prayer written by the state board of regents to *Almighty God* contradicted their religious beliefs. *Incidentally, they were supported by several religious groups* (five other plaintiffs) including rabbinical organizations: three Jews and two self-proclaimed spiritual individuals who opposed to the school prayer: *Almighty God, we acknowledge our dependence upon Thee, and we beg Thy blessings upon us, our parents, our teachers and our country, Amen* (Wikipedia, 2015c). *Have Mercy, God is worthy of all praises!*

Howbeit, the American Jewish Committee, the Synagogue Council of America, and the American Ethical Union joined on behalf of the plaintiffs and submitted briefs urging the court to rule that the prayer was unconstitutional (Wikipedia, 2015c). One could challenge "A little leaven, leaveneth the whole lump" (Galatians 5:9). After the decision was made favoring the Engel et al case, others followed. In the *Wallace v. Jaffree* (1985) case, the Supreme Court ruled Alabama's law permitting one minute for prayer or meditation was unconstitutional. In the *Lee v. Weisman* (1992) case, the court prohibited clergy-led prayer at middle schools' graduation ceremonies (Wikipedia, 2015c). Incidentally, the *Lee v. Weisman* case was a basis for the *Santa Fe ISD v. Doe* (2000) case, in which the Court extended the ban to school-organized *student*-led prayer at high school football games (Wikipedia, 2015c).

In addition, one school (Dr. Hamman Elementary School in Taber, Alberta; population approximately 8,000) continued to allow prayer in school up until 2013, until one parent (Ms. Bell; an agnostic) complained that when her two children heard the prayer they became anxious and came home crying. The principle of the school removed prayer from the school because of Ms. Bell's complaint. Praise God, many parents of this particular school are still fighting to have prayer reinstated (Baklinski, 2013). But what are we as Christians doing to reinstate prayer in our children and grandchildren schools? Are we banning together, or are we just standing by the wayside doing nothing? Amazingly, God always has somebody working on His behalf.

Recently two cheerleader squads defied a Tennessee school district decision to ban prayer at football games after receiving complaints from the American Civil Liberties Union (ACLU) and Freedom from Religion Foundation (FFRF). By the way, neither of the foundations had ever objected to any Muslim public prayers. The ACLU and FFRF sent the Oneida Special School District a threatening letter complaining about school-sanctioned prayers over the loud-speaker at football games (DeWitt, 2014). Again, the principle of the school removed prayer and replaced it with a moment of silence. Even so, one cheerleader of Oneida (in defense of her religious faith) voiced that with various troubles faced in their community on a daily basis, prayer was very much needed.

After the moment of silence, with heads bowed and hands joined together (with other cheerleaders and the opponent's team cheerleaders), she begin reciting the Lord's Prayer. Amazingly, before the prayer was over, the entire audience (with heads bowed) in the stadium joined in with the cheerleaders in prayer (DeWitt, 2014). *Praise God, for prayer is the key to the Kingdom!* While it is devastating that audible prayer has been removed from our schools, truly no one can stop our children from praying inwardly and spreading Agape love. We must continue to teach our children to love and pray without ceasing even when the love is not returned. For all can attest, since the removal of prayer in our schools the nation has experienced downfalls. Prayer nationwide is gravely needed in our homes, schools, workplaces, and churches.

Certainly, we are living in perilous times in which men have become self-pleasers, warriors against the brethren, and feel there's no need for prayer. But what have we as Christians done to offset these behaviors? Have we become lovers of the world and have turned away from God? Have we been deceived and are now serving other gods? Psalm 41:9, English Standard Version (ESV) states "Even my close friend in whom I trusted, who ate my bread, has lifted his heel against me. We as a nation need to show more love and pray congruently like never before; for prayer changes things. Praise God for individuals who know and teach others the significance of Agape love and continuous prayer. Two individuals in the past (in my humble opinion) were good examples of prayer warriors.

Mother Teresa and Mahatma Gandhi were prayer warriors and demonstrated Agape love. What did these individuals speak on concerning prayer? One of Mother Teresa's famous quotes states "Keep the joy of loving God in your heart and share this joy with all you meet especially your family. Be holy-let us pray" (Ewtn, n.d.). Gandhi posits, "Prayer is not asking. It is a longing of the soul. It is daily admission of one's weakness. It is better in prayer to have a heart without words than words without a heart" (Goodreads 2015). Mother Teresa and Gandhi posit that prayer is gravely needed in our society and without prayer individuals, couples, and families are left to their own resources, which are meager. Yet, when we plug into God who is the powerhouse of prayer, we are enlightened, strengthened and equipped by the Holy Spirit to do works that would be impossible for people like us with limited intelligence, insight and creative ability (Ma, 2009).

Nationwide, Christian prayer warriors should come together and petition God as intercessors concerning the downfalls of our society. Let us pray to God in relationship to ceasing crime, violence, hatred in our homes, families, and society as a whole. For we know that only God can replace this negativity with love. If churches (the called-out) do not band together to pray for our nation, who will? A modern proverb with unknown authorship eloquently states: *If you don't stand for something, you'll fall for anything*

(Word Press, 2014). Let us wake up, for it does not take a rocket scientist to denote our nation is in dire need of love and healing, not hatred as exemplified. According to Calloway (2013):

> Our world is plagued with senseless crime and violence. Pervasive hate crimes, bullying, sexual assaults, and murders all signify a world where the precious life of our neighbor is neither cherished nor honored, neither valued nor respected. In this world, it seems that the precious life of our neighbor is perceived as nothing more than an object worthy of petty thievery. . . For all of its usual boisterousness, the Church (universal) has said and done little to stop gun violence, especially in communities of color. We know why those who make money working in concert with gun manufacturers are silent, but why the Church and especially why the Black Church? But even more than our silence, other than homilies that bemoan the problem and offer few or no solutions, our failure to act (get off the sidelines) has been difficult to fathom and hard to reconcile with the *love* we say we have for God, for black and brown people, and for black and brown children in particular (p.1).

Our society are filled with so much hatred that love appears to be a foreign language; with the exception of the giving spirit exhibited during the Christmas holiday, *help us Lord!* Societal hatred toward various cultures is noteworthy in the United States. According to Dr. Demetrius E. Ford, Ph.D., J.D.,

Psy.D., (2015) as cited in SPLC, 2013, there are numerous hate groups that currently exist in the United States. In fact, as of 2012 there were about 1,012: 196 neo-Nazi, 186 separate Ku Klux Klan (KKK), 113 Black Separatist, and 111 White Nationalist. There are 98 White Power Skinheads, 93 neo-Confederate, 39 Christian identities, and 90 General hate groups; anti-gay, Holocaust denial, racist music, radical traditionalist Catholic and others (Ford, 2015). Unfortunately, hatred has been present since the beginning of time and will remain until Our Savior Jesus Christ returns. Yet, we as Christians can find love, peace, happiness, joy, and much more in Jesus if we just return to Him and repent of our sins. God is an Awesome God and he longs to have you as His child; return back to Him.

For, God is patience and in due time He transforms us into a newness of light that represents the love of Christ (Lucado, 2015). However, do we love God or the world? Although we say we love God, many have become misguided upon viewing various wrongful lifestyles enacted via mass media which deceive them into believing they should do what they want to do regardless of the Word of God and His commandments. Often in our youth, many cultures practice their choice of religion, beliefs, observances, while following various traditions. Nevertheless, the question is asked, is the love of the True and Only Living God exemplified in our lives, homes, and away from home? Are we serving God or Mammon? Do people really see the love of God in us? Do we love our brothers and sisters as God has commanded us? Do we have a heart to forgive our brothers as Jesus instructed 70 x7 (Matthew 18:22)?   Are our lights shining as a beacon drawing others to God?   Proverbs 4:18 reminds us that . . . "the path of the just is as the shining light that shineth more and more unto the perfect day." (Psalms 84: 11) states, "For the LORD God is a sun and shield: the LORD will give grace and glory: no good thing will he withhold from them that walk uprightly."   If we love God, we will keep His statures and abide by His commandments; most importantly the commandment to love others, for love conquers all.   Need we be reminded?   Let us return to our First Love (Jesus Christ) and exemplify Agape Love always.

CHAPTER 6
AGAPE LOVE IN ACTION

As with many churches of today, the churches in Revelations 2-3 (with the exception of Philadelphia), Jesus praised, chastised, and instructed to humbly repent and return eagerly to their First Love or except the consequences.   God does not appreciate slothfulness rendered in His services. We as Christians are in a spiritual warfare against principalities, powers, rulers of darkness of this world, and against spiritual wickedness in high places (Ephesians 6:12); not against our Lord and Savior whom we say we love.

Agape love purifies the soul and causes one to be obedient to the truth, and this divine love causes one to have sincere brotherly love for one another with a pure heart (1st Peter 1:22).

One in accepting/believing in Jesus Christ, constantly studying the Word of God, and exhibiting God in their daily walk are purified through the Holy Spirit and can sincerely share brotherly love. 1st John 4:7 (NIV), declares, "Dear friends, let us love one another, for love comes from God. Everyone who loves has been born of God and knows God."   Schaefer (1996) contends, "God Is Love, Agape . . . the love theme of the Bible, can only be defined by the nature of God" (p. 1). God loves everyone regardless of their faults, He will never condemn you, for there is ". . . no condemnation to them which are in Christ Jesus, who walk not after the flesh, but after the Spirit" (Romans 8:1). Just as Jesus loves us, let us love one another regardless if love isn't reciprocated.

Jesus reminds all in Luke 6: 32-35, "For if ye love them which love you, what thank have ye? For sinners also love those that love them. And if ye do good to them which do good to you, what thank have ye? For sinners also do even the same. And if ye lend to them of whom ye hope to receive, what thank have ye? For sinners also lend to sinners, to receive as much again. But love ye your enemies, and do good, and lend, hoping for nothing again; and your reward shall be great, and ye shall be the children of the Highest: for he is kind unto the unthankful and to the evil."

Powerful, while these passages of scriptures may appear likely for some, others may find these commandments to be most difficult, specifically when one does harm to another; leaving a deepen soreness in one's heart such as murdering a loved one. Truly, one would consider this individual an enemy. Yet, Jesus states in Matthew 5: 44, "But I say unto you, love your enemies, bless them that curse you, do good to them that hate you, and pray for them which despitefully use you, and persecute you. . ." In essence, no matter what the circumstances, we must always do what is right in the sight of God.

The Word of God speaks of two women (in my modest opinion) who showed evidence of Agape love.

These two women were Mary (the mother of Jesus) and Elizabeth (the mother of John the Baptist). Because of Mary's obedience to God she was blessed in giving birth to our Lord and Savior Jesus Christ. In addition, Mary is known throughout the world as blessed and highly favored among women (Luke 1:26-28). While some decide to follow and serve God upon reaching mid-age or older, Mary decided to serve and be obedient to God in her youth. According to Chilton (2011), Mary was around 13 years of age, the age in which Jewish maidens married in that time. Mary made this decision in spite of: being ridiculed, what Joseph her betrothed husband felt, and possibly being stoned to death (Chilton, 2011). Unknown to some, Mary's son Jesus (our Lord and Savior) was also mocked as being born of a fornicator (John 8:41). Mary's response to the angel of the Lord was powerful, she stated, "Behold the handmaid of the Lord; be it unto me according to thy word" (Luke 1:38). Mary's obedience to God at such a young age mirrored a stronghold youth with Agape love.

Elizabeth (Mary's cousin) also demonstrated Agape love by being faithful and obedient to God. After being barren for many years Elizabeth became pregnant (at an old age) with her son John the Baptist; forerunner to Jesus. In fact, when Mary informed Elizabeth concerning her pregnancy with our Lord and Savior, Elizabeth's son in utero (John the Baptist) leaped and Elizabeth was filed the Holy Spirit (Luke 1:41). We all know the story of what happened to John the Baptist; truly he served God to the end of his days. Jesus stated in Matthew 11:11, "Verily I say unto you, among them that are born of women there hath not risen a greater than John the Baptist . . ."

While society is in an uproar, we all can relate to individuals God has used in the past and present for His purpose. One individual that comes to mind who exemplified Agape love was Mother Teresa. Born as Gonxha Agnes Bojaxhiu in Skopje, Yugoslavia, Mother Teresa was a well-to-do compassionate Catholic missionary, who for more than 50 years rendered strenuous, physical, emotional, and spiritual work to the less fortunate individuals. Although much of her younger years were centered in the church, it wasn't until she reached the age of 18 that she decided to become a nun. While attending school in a protected environment for the daughters of the wealthy, her new *vocation* developed and grew (Guntzelman, 2015).

Mother Teresa taught history and geography with dedication and enjoyment for 15 years. After attending the novitiate (training/probation period) of the Sisters of Loreto in Darjeeling while on a retreat, she made her first vows and adopted the name *Teresa*, honoring both saints; Teresa of Avila and Therese of Lisieux and begin her years of service to God's people. Later she was commission by God to leave this position and follow Christ into the slums to serve Him among the poorest of the poor" (Guntzelman, 2015), in which she obeyed until her health failed. Mother Teresa spoke many words of wisdom; one favorite of mine is titled *Doing Right*, in which we all can emulate (Sayings, n. d.):

There should be less talk; a preaching point is not a meeting point. What do you do then?

Take a broom and clean someone's house. That says enough.

People are often unreasonable, illogical, and self centered; forgive them anyway. If you are kind, people may accuse you of selfish, ulterior motives; Be kind anyway. If you are successful you will win some false friends and true enemies: Succeed anyway. If you are honest and frank, people may cheat you; Be honest and frank anyway. What you spend years building, someone could destroy overnight; Build anyway. If you find serenity and happiness, they may be jealous; Be happy anyway. The good you do today, people will often forget tomorrow; Do good anyway. Give the world the best you have, and it may never be enough; Give the world the best you've got anyway. You see, in the final analysis, it is between you and God; it was never between you and them anyway (p. 1).

Doing right towards others in spite of their disposition is always the precise thing to do. Nevertheless, we as a society have become desensitized to our brothers and sisters (those considered normal and even more so to those considered abnormal). Truly, all people deserve to be loved and cared for effectively. In demonstrating Agape love an individual's status by no means should determine how they are treated. Witnessing individuals of lower status, substance abuse, mental disorders, and other problems being mistreated on the streets is heartbreaking, but to see these individuals being mistreated in our churches is devastating. We as Christians (the Body of Christ) are to be examples for the lost sheep and assist them in coming to Christ (Luke 15:3-10) because we love the brethren (1st John 3:14) and we dare not lead them astray because of their mishaps.

The Bible instructs us to love everyone (John 13:34) and treat all as we desire to be treated (Matthew 7:12). The question is asked again, are we showing Agape love towards our brothers and sisters who are considered normal and abnormal? We are living in a society in which many of our brothers and sisters are bound and addicted to substance abuse (drugs and alcohol), have we as Christians tried to assist them in into recovery by petitioning/fighting with Congress on their behalf in gaining medical assistance? According to Open Society Institute (2010), one in every 10 (2.6 million) Americans over the age of 12 are addicted to drugs and alcohol resulting in 23.5 million addicted Americans in the United States. Yet, only 11 percent are receiving treatment while others do not have access to treatment due to *no health coverage insurance*.

Banning together and fighting with the Government for Health Care Reform will provide healthcare for all. Many Americans are battling with mental health issues and are not receiving help due to our Government closing the doors of mental health institutions, leaving our brothers and sisters wandering on the streets. In fact, the National Institute of Mental Health (NIMH) when applied to the 2004 U. S. Census residential population found that 57.7 million

Americans, approximately 26.2 percent being 18 years of age and older (one in four adults) are diagnosed and suffers from mental disorders in a given year (The Kim Foundation, 2014).

This includes individual with mood disorders, who commit suicide, have schizophrenia, anxiety disorders, panic disorder, obsessive-compulsive disorder (OCD), generalized anxiety disorder (GAD), social phobia, eating disorders (anorexia nervosa, bulimia nervosa, and binge-eating), attention deficit hyperactivity disorder (ADHD), autism, and Alzheimer's Disease (The Kim Foundation, 2014). Individuals with mood disorders accounted for approximately 20.9 percent million adults (9.5 percent of the U.S. population 18 and older in a given year). Suicide, in the United States accounted for more than 90 percent of individuals with a mental disorder. In 2004, approximately 32, 439 (11 per 100,000) individuals died by suicide (The Kim Foundation, 2014). Schizophrenia: approximately 2-4 million America (1.1 percent of the population age 18 and over given a year) are diagnosed. Anxiety Disorders: approximately 40 million adults 18 and older (18.1 percent) are diagnosed. Panic Disorder: approximately 6 million Americans 18 and older (2.2 percent of people in this age group) are diagnosed (The Kim Foundation, 2014).

Obsessive-Compulsive Disorder (OCD): approximately 2.2 million American adults age 18 and older (1.0 percent of people in this age group) have OCD. Post-Traumatic Stress Disorder (PSTD): approximately 7.7 million Americans adults age 18 and older (3.5 percent of people in this age group) have

PTSD (The Kim Foundation, 2014). Generalized anxiety disorder (GAD): approximately 6.8 million American adults (3.1 percent of people in this age group) have GAD. Social phobia: approximately 15 million American adults (6.8 percent of people in this age group) have social phobias (The Kim Foundation, 2014). Eating Disorders (anorexia nervosa, bulimia nervosa, and binge-eating): Anorexia nervosa 0.5 to 3.7 females suffer from anorexia, 35 percent of those with binge-eating disorders, and 1.1 to 4.2 percent suffer from bulimia disorders. Attention Deficit Hyperactivity Disorder (ADHD): common in children and adolescents, however, affects approximately 4.1 percent of adults ages 18-44 in a given year (The Kim Foundation, 2014). Autism: In 3-10 years of age are approximately 3.4 cases per 1000 children, and is about four times common in boys than girls. Alzheimer's disease: The number of Americans affected with Alzheimer's disease (approximately 4.5 Million) since 1980 and is common among the age group 65 and older (The Kim Foundation, 2014). Our society is in need of love and a spiritual healing; let us pray to God for healing and sustainability of our nation, in addition to us spreading Agape love.

Realistically, we cannot holistically reach and care for all the poor, sickly, and needy nationwide, we can however reach and teach the ones that are nearby. We as Christians can go a step further in petitioning our politicians via: technology, mass media, in person, and letters in support of sufficient programs for our sisters and brothers in need of effective treatment plans and organizations. True love shows action as one does in caring gently for their children by: unconditionally loving, feeding, clothing, educating, and protecting them without fear. "Herein is our love made perfect, that we may have boldness in the day of Judgement: because as he is, so are we in the world. There is no fear in love; but perfect love casteth out fear: because fear hath torment. He that feareth is not made perfect in love" (1st John 4: 17-18).

Henry (2015) in paraphrasing Leviticus 19:17 and Philippians 2:4 posits, "Those who are unconcerned in the affairs of their brethren and take no care when they have opportunity to prevent their hurt in their bodies, goods, or good name, especially in their souls, do in effect speak Cain's language." *Powerful!* Let us pray to God for boldness, a forgiving heart, and a spirit that exhibits Agape Love to assist our brothers and sisters in need and prayerfully lead them to Christ. Yet, many of us (yes, even Christians) find it hard to forgive and hold grudges not just against our Christians brothers and sister but against our biological family members as well. We must fervently pray to God to help us forgive and move forward in brotherly love.

Agape Love Forgives

Truly God is a forgiving God as exemplified through Him giving us His Son Jesus Christ to die for our sins. Jesus showed Agape Love and forgiveness even at His death. He stated to His Father to forgive them for they know not what they do; while they tore off His clothing and cast lots to divide them (Luke 23:34). Although Jesus' disciple Peter denied Him *three times before the crucifixion,* Jesus forgave him. *Great is Agape Love!* Jesus asked Peter *after His resurrection three times* if he loved him (John 21:15–17). Jesus forgave Peter to the point of building His Church upon Peter's confession (Matthew 16:18). Jesus also looked beyond two of His other disciples' faults (James and John, the sons of Zebedee; known as the sons of Thunder; Mark 3:17) while they were being aggressive (Luke 9:54) and self-centered (Mark 10:35-37). Jesus saw their needs and forgave them.

James and John on the other hand were not as forgiving, in Luke 9:54 instead of forgiving the people in Samaria for not accepting the message of Jesus, they wanted to summons fire from heaven to devour them. Furthermore, the two brothers instead of feeling remorseful upon hearing of the foretelling of Jesus' betrayal and brutal death in Mark 10:35-37, were only concerned about having seats of recognition in Heaven. But there is healing through Agape love, and because of Jesus' unconditional love for these three disciples they eventually turned from their ungodly ways and preached the Word of God until their deaths. Two of these disciples were martyred. In fact, James was the first disciple to be martyred (murdered with a sword; Acts 12:1-19) and Peter, by his request was crucified upside down. John was the only original disciple to reach old age and die peacefully in Patmos (Kiger, 2015).

The sons of Zebedee and Peter played a significant role as disciples of Jesus and was privileged (Matthew 26:37, Mark 5:37, Mark 13:3, Mark 14:32-33) versus other disciples in eye witnessing the transfiguration (Mark 9:2). Christians in recognizing the leadership of Jesus must show love, compassion, and forgiveness to all mankind. Our brothers and sisters, in particular those shackled with worldly issues: habitual addictions, substance abuse, incarceration, and other problems gravely need our love, forgiveness, and assistance. When we show love and forgiveness for our brothers and sisters, we show the love of God; for none of us are sinless or exempted from future sins. Let us come together blindly as little children playing together (diverse cultures) without a care as to what one's past or present situation may be, how a person looks, what a person have or have not, and whether a person is a sinner or not.

The fact remains, we all have sinned, yet we are God's children and He continues to love and forgive us. God gave us His Son, Jesus Christ as our atonement for our sins. John reminds us in 1st John 2:1-6 (ESV), "My little children, I am writing these things to you so that you may not sin. But if anyone does sin, we have an advocate with the Father, Jesus Christ the righteous. He is the propitiation for our sins, and not for ours only but also for the sins of the whole world. And by this we know that we have come to know him, if we keep his commandments. Whoever says *I know him* but does not keep his commandments is a liar, and the truth is not in him, but whoever keeps his word, in him truly the love of God is perfected. By this we may know that we are in him; whoever says he abides in him ought to walk in the same way in which he walked." Great is the power of Agape love; but how does one acquire and retain Agape love? For surely if one have

Agape love; Philia, Storge, and Eros love will be of no quandary. Let us fervently pray to God to acquire Agape love in our hearts.

Acquiring Agape Love

The principal steps in acquiring Agape love are to believe, confess, accept Jesus Christ as your personal Savior, and repent (turn away from) of one's sins. Ezekiel 14: 6 instructs readers to, ". . .Repent, and turn yourselves from your idols, and turn away from your faces from all your abominations. One must then be baptized which requires being dipped under the water as Jesus was baptized by John the Baptist (Matthew 3: 13-16), and obey the statues of the Lord. Still one cannot gain the true meaning of love without gaining *wisdom* about God who is the Authenticator of Agape Love. Yet, what is wisdom? According to Wikipedia (2015b), "Wisdom is the ability to think and act using knowledge, experience, understanding, common sense, and insight . . . Wisdom is a habit or disposition to perform the action with the highest degree of adequacy under any given circumstance" (p.1).

The Word of God states in Psalm 111:10 that "The fear of the LORD *is the beginning of wisdom*: a good understanding have all they that do his commandments: his praise endureth for ever." Job an upright man of God, who was challenged by Satan himself confirms this statement, "And unto man he said, behold, the fear of the Lord, that is wisdom; and to depart from evil is understanding" (Job 28:28). The Bible instructs us to keep the statues and commandments of God without adding or takings from them. Deuteronomy 4:6 states "Keep therefore and do them; for this is your wisdom and your understanding in the sight of the nations, which shall hear all these statutes, and say, surely this great nation is a wise and understanding people."

Wisdom is a gift from God in allowing one to discern any given information. Merriam-Webster (2015b) defines wisdom as the ability to discern things that most individuals do not understand through natural ability, gained knowledge or experiences. Yet, what if one is following the statues of God but still lacks wisdom, and how can wisdom be gained? Let's see what the Word of God says concerning this matter; James 1:5 (NIV) states, "If any of you lacks wisdom, you should ask God, who gives generously to all without finding fault, and it will be given to you."

Solomon, the son of King David in showing love for God by being obedient to his father's instructions visited Gibeon and offered a thousand burnt offerings on the altar to the Lord. While visiting Gibeon, the Lord appeared to Solomon in a dream asking him *whatever he wanted He would give it to him*. Solomon in turn praised God for showing greatness to his father King David (a servant of the Lord) because of his faithfulness to the Lord, righteous and upright in heart, and for allowing him (a servant of the Lord) to become the King in his father's place. Yet, Solomon in being a child informed God that he did not know how to carry out the duties as a king over a great number of people (too many to count) and asked God for a discerning heart to govern God's people and to distinguish between right and wrong.

God being pleased with Solomon's answer of asking for discernment in implementing justice and not longevity, wealth, or the death of his enemies, not only gave him a discerning heart and wisdom, but wealth and honor. God informed Solomon that there will never be one as wise as him and God promised Solomon longevity if he would remain obedient to Him (1st Kings 3:1-15, NIV). Some theologians believe Solomon was 12 years of age when he was coronated as king, reigned 40 years, and died at 53 due to disobedience to God (Hirsch, Price, Bacher, Seligsohn, Montgomery, & Toy, 2011). Just as Solomon, we can ask God for wisdom and discernment in acquiring Agape love which should be a desire of all Christian's hearts. God will give you the desires of your heart when you are submissive and acknowledge Him in all thy ways (Psalms 37:4); He wants all to acquire Agape Love. Still we must remain steadfast in God for preservation of Agape Love.

Maintaining Agape Love

Agape love in being so powerful requires one to continue in daily prayer to God for the retention of the anointing of His love. We as Christians are to pray without ceasing. In times like these, who can afford *not to pray* continuously? How blessed we are to be able to pray to God for ourselves because of His Agape love in allowing His only begotten son Jesus (the only perfect sacrifice) the Highest Preeminent Priest to die for the remission of our sins. *Thank you Lord*, we do not have to confess our sins to priests (Hebrews 9), we can go to God in prayer for ourselves in fervent prayer. We must have a sincere heart and not pray in amiss, in formulae, or for gain glory of people (Matthew 6:7).

Let us pray with Agape love. Parishioners in Christ must have the love of God in their hearts not exhibiting jealousy towards one another as we see in many congregations of today's society. No one can get a prayer through if they have hostility against another. We must make amends with our brothers and sisters in which we find fault before we kneel to God in prayer. In maintaining Agape love we must remain humble and not become puffed up; for God does not like the proud. In representing the body of Christ, we as Christians must love without ceasing and always have a forgiving heart. Holding grudges is not Christ-like, for when you forgive individuals who have done you wrong, God continues to forgive you. The same being when you do not forgive those who have wronged you; God will not forgive the wrong you have done to others (Matthew 6: 14-15). Love causes one to forgive, and forgiveness brings about healing. While love is manifested as a beautiful feeling, love can also result in hurt and pain; nevertheless, love conquers all.

CHAPTER 7
HEALING OF THE NATION

We as Christians must strive diligently in keeping unity in representation of the body of Christ, *in* and *out* of Sunday morning worship services; always spreading Agape love. Christians in representing unity and retention of Agape love draws others to Christ as we die daily to the flesh (Philippians 2: 1-11) which continuously fights against the Spirit (Galatians 5:17). Our faith and love brings unity which is strengthened by the Word of God and His spirit which lives inside of us. Staying in prayer daily and communicating with *God the Father* keeps Christians from becoming puffed up and alerts their remembrance of not being exempted from the wiles of Satan. As a member of the body of Christ and emulating the ways of our Lord and Savior Jesus Christ through Agape Love, there is no room for pride. Pride in itself is an abomination to God, for it was pride that caused Satan to be cast out of Heaven (Revelation 12:7-12).

Unfortunately, the world is eager to promote the proud and grants them wealth from their proud dispositions. Nonetheless, *Glory be to God* who teaches us in His Word in 1st John 2:16, "For all that is in the world, the lust of the flesh, and the lust of the eyes, and the pride of life, is not of the Father, but is of the world." Proverbs 16:18 confirms, "Pride goes before destruction, and a haughty spirit before a fall." Pride leads to division and conflict (Proverbs 13:10) which is not of God. Pride has no room for love, in particularly, Agape love.

Agape love is sustained by continuing to engulf the Word of God, listening to His teachings from spiritual leaders and saints, while staying steadfast in prayer. If we as Christians do not know how to pray, we must appeal to God for assistance in this matter. Submitting ourselves in prayer shows our reverence to God, keeps us humble toward Him, assists us in trouncing temptations, and strengthens our intellect. After we pray, we must spend time to listen and reflect on what God shares with us through His Holy Spirit. Some things God enlightens us on should be shared with our Christian brothers and sisters for their edification; for there is strength in unity. Agape love is so powerful that we should want all of our brothers and sisters in Christ to be empowered with this love, for as Christians the Holy Spirit is suppose to reside in us (2nd Timothy 1:14). I strongly believe that if we as Christians are empowered with Agape love, we will draw non-Christians into the body of Christ. God in demonstrating Agape love shows the significance of His love in being absolute and amazingly universal.

Retention of Agape love does not mean that we as Christians will never be provoked to anger, but we must pray to sin not (Ephesians 4:26). Maintenance of Agape love does not mean that we as

Christians will never fall down, but if we do, we must pray to get back up (Matthew 6:14). Preservation of Agape love does not mean that everyone will love and accept you, yet we Christians must love everyone (John 13:34; Matthews 5:44). Christians emulating Agape love shows our new birth as accepting Jesus Christ as our Lord and Savior, its shows that we accept being ". . . buried with him by baptism into death: its shows that as Christ was raised up from the dead by the glory of the Father, even so we also should walk in newness of life" (Romans. 6: 4).

We as Christians walking in newness of life must treat our families with *Storge love* and show ourselves to be friendly (*Philia love*) amongst the brethrens. The Bible in Proverbs 18: 24, posits, "A man that hath friends must show himself friendly: and there is a friend that sticketh closer than a brother. We as Christians must continue in brotherly love (Heb. 13: 1). In being obedient to God, *Eros love* will follow and the bed will be undefiled. For God said in His Holy word, "Delight thyself also in the LORD: and he shall give thee the desires of thine heart. Commit thy way unto the LORD; trust also in him; and he shall bring it to pass" (Psalm 37: 4-5). The question is: As a nation, under God, do we want Agape Love, or are we content being rebellious against Him?

A Rebellious Nation

For centuries we as a nation have been rebellious against God, yet affirm we desire world peace, but there is no true peace without God! "For rebellion is as the sin of witchcraft, and stubbornness is as iniquity and idolatry. Because thou hast rejected the word of the Lord . . ." (1st Samuel 15:23). One scholar (Parnell, 2015) denotes:

> America as a nation has turned its back on the Lord God Jehovah. This can clearly be seen in the ungodly antics of the politicians and the sinful demands of its citizenry. As a result, America's politicians and millions of its citizens, according to the Word of God, will incur the wrath of God at some point in time. Of course, most politicians and any other persons who have rebelled against the commandments of God would label anyone who suggested such an outrageous assumption as being mentally disturbed or maybe even psycho. But, despite what gainsayers would say, the Bible clearly states the destiny of such rebellious people who have put God on the back burner in exchange for freedom to do anything that they so desire. In Psalm 9:17, King David, the writer of most of the Psalms and who was inspired of the Holy Spirit, states that the wicked shall be turned into hell, and all the nations that forget God (p.1).

Nevertheless, we remain a rebellious nation and continue to have lustful desires (James 1:14) of the world. Ezekiel 2:8 confirms our rebellious nature in stating, "But thou, son of man, hear what I say unto thee; be not thou rebellious like that rebellious house: open thy mouth, and eat that I give thee." Still God, even in our rebellious and sinful nature loves us and longs for us to return to Him. Thank you Lord for being longsuffering (Numbers 14:18). We as Christians know that God is able to do all things and He loves man regardless of their faults. *The Power of Agape Love* can change our sinful nature and give us a new spirit that will serve the *One and Only True God.*

"For as many are led by the Spirit of God they are the sons of God" (Romans 8:14). Jesus states in John 4:24, "God is a spirit; and they that worship Him must worship Him in spirit and in truth." The truth concerning our Lord and Savior Jesus Christ must originate in our homes, be reinforced in our churches, uplifted in our schools, freely exercised on our jobs, and expressed in our communities. Yes, we as a nation have turned away from God and forgotten the *Power of Agape Love* because of our fleshly selfish worldly desires. For we are penalized or prosecuted if we chastise our children, if we pray out loud in public places, if we dare speak of abominations in the site of God. Yet, when calamities strike our nation we then run to the church as reported in increased church attendance and increase in the sale of Bibles after the 911attacks.

In spite of multi-religious groups and churches, Agape or philia love is seldom seen. Truly, a change must take place in our nation; we as a society have become self-pleasers, desensitized to others, and rebellious against God. Howbeit, the Bible forewarns us concerning this change due to sin and states, "And because iniquity shall abound, the love of many shall wax cold" (Matthew 24: 12). Compassion for one another has been lost; we have become impatient and angry. What happened to being humble like Jesus?

Especially Christians, we are taught to be humble and to communicate with care.

For we know to "Be not deceived: evil communications corrupt good manners (1st Corinthians 15:33), and that "A soft answer turneth away wrath (anger, rage, fury): but grievous (awful, dire, dreadful, terrible) words stir up anger. The tongue of the wise useth knowledge aright: but the mouth of fools poureth out foolishness" (Proverbs 15:1). Let us not be like the heathens in expressing anger towards our brothers and sisters, let us strive to retain and spread the *Power of Agape love*; not only during the holidays or when calamities strike, but always.

Without a doubt, we as Christians are disturbed with the disorders of this world but we must continue to love one another: remembering we are in the world but not of the world (Romans 12:2). We must continue to treat all with respect, do all things decent, in order, and pleasing to God. While it is normal for our fleshly bodies to become angry with the sins of the world, we dare not go against God's statutes. For God will have the last say as He states in His Word, "Dearly beloved, avenge not yourselves, but rather give place unto wrath: for it is written, vengeance is mine; I will repay, saith the Lord. Therefore if thine enemy hunger, feed him; if he thirst, give him drink: for in so doing thou shalt heap coals of fire on his head. Be not overcome of evil, but overcome evil with good (Romans 12: 19-21). Hence, we as servants of God must continue to imitate Christ and exhibit Agape love to all in spite of their short comings.

Agape Love is Contagious

Agape love is powerful and contagious when shared with others. With all the turmoil and havoc faced in today's' society one could argue the world greatly needs Agape love and is foolish not to turn from our wicked ways and run to God for the healing of our nation. Church leaders and parishioners nationwide must ban together joining forces with community coalitions (putting our differences aside) to fight against violence and havoc in our communities and hold our political leaders (chosen by us) accountable for enacting laws that strongly go against the ordinance of God. According to Dr. Martin Luther King Jr., "The ultimate tragedy is not the oppression and cruelty by the bad people but the silence over that by the good people" (Brainy Quote, 2015).

Now that we are savvy with our hi-tech electronics and have speedy access to the World Wide Web (via computers, androids, iphones, ipads, etc.) and social media (Face book, Twitter, etc.), let us employ them to contact our political leaders (available 24/7) to voice our concerns regarding the havoc in our society. For we; the called-out are soldiers in the army of the Lord. Let us put our war clothes on, and as stated in Ephesians 6:10-18, (NIV):

> Finally, be strong in the Lord and in his mighty power. *Put on the full armor of God*, so that you can take your stand against the devil's schemes. For our struggle is not against flesh and blood, but against the rulers, against the authorities, against the powers of this dark world and against the spiritual forces of evil in

the heavenly realms. Therefore *put on the full armor of God,* so that when the day of evil comes, you may be able to stand your ground, and after you have done everything, to stand. Stand firm then, with the *belt of truth* buckled around your waist, with the *breastplate of righteousness* in place, and with your *feet fitted with the readiness that comes from the gospel of peace.* In addition to all this, take up the *shield of faith,* with which you can extinguish all the flaming arrows of the evil one. Take the *helmet of salvation* and the *sword of the Spirit,* which is the word of God. And pray in the Spirit on all occasions with all kinds of prayers and requests. With this in mind, be alert and always keep on praying for all the Lord's people.

Conclusions

Christians are the light of the world. Jesus confirms this in Matthew 5:14-16 by stating, "Ye are the light of the world. A city that is set on a hill cannot be hid. Neither do men light a candle, and put it under a bushel, but on a candlestick; and it giveth light unto all that are in the house. Let your light so shine before men, that they may see your good works, and glorify your Father which is in heaven." Even in a world full of darkness our lights must shine, for "Darkness cannot drive out darkness: only light can do that. Dr. Martin Luther King Jr. postulated that "Hate cannot drive out hate: only love can do that" (Brainy Quote, 2015).

The love of God must begin in the home, we as

parents must teach our children at an early age about God and His Agape love. Let us bring our children to church (not send them) to assist them in learning more about our Lord and Savior Jesus Christ and the significance of forgiving and loving others. When we encounter individuals who display hatred and despair in their hearts, let's show them love, in particular God's Love, and how He welcomes everyone. Let us come together as the body of Christ (universal church) in standing up for what is right in the sight of God. We must put aside our differences; humble ourselves, come together in unity, and pray to God for the betterment of our nation.

His word states, "If my people, which are called by my name, shall humble themselves, and pray, and seek my face, and turn from their wicked ways; then will I hear from heaven, and will forgive their sin, and will heal their land" (2nd Chronicles 7:14). We were born to serve God, not material wealth or possessions, and our duty as Christians is to win souls for the Lord. While the world offer temporary fame and fortune, it cannot give love, joy, peace, contentment, or eternal life. Jesus states in Matthew 16: 26, "For what is a man profited, if he shall gain the whole world, and lose his own soul? Or what shall a man give in exchange for his soul?" One in acquiring and retaining Agape love can look forward to eternal life in Heaven with our Lord and Savior Jesus Christ; *that's powerful!*

For this vary reason, Jesus came down from heaven to become the ultimate perfect sacrifice for our sins (Colossians 1:22;1 Peter 1:19). Through Him, the promise of life eternal with God becomes effective through faith to those who believe as epitomized in Galatians 3:22, "But the scripture hath concluded all under sin, that the promise by faith of Jesus Christ might be given to them that believe." These two words; *faith* and *believing* are significant to our salvation. It is through our believing in the shedding of Christ's blood for our sins, and that He rose for our justification that we receive eternal life. "For by grace are ye saved through faith; and that not of yourselves: it is the gift of God: Not of works, lest any man should boast" (Ephesians 2:8-9). Let us continue to share Agape love towards one another; for Love is the greatest gift from God and without love we have nothing. Paul wrote in 1st Corinthians 13: 1-8 (EXB):

> Though I speak with the tongues of men and of angels, but have not love, I have become sounding brass or a clanging cymbal. And though I have the gift of prophecy, and understand all mysteries and all knowledge, and though I have all faith, so that I could remove mountains, but have not love, I am nothing. And though I bestow all my goods to feed the poor, and though I give my body to be burned, but have not love, it profits me nothing. Love suffers long and is kind; love does not envy; love does not parade itself, is not puffed up; does not behave rudely, does not seek its own, is not provoked, thinks no evil; does not rejoice in iniquity, but rejoices in the truth; bears all things, believes all things, hopes all things, endures all things. Love never fails. But whether there are prophecies, they will fail;

whether there are tongues, they will cease; whether there is knowledge, it will vanish away. For we know in part and we prophesy in part, But when that which is perfect has come, then that which is in part will be done away. . . And now abide faith, hope, love, these three; but the greatest of these is love (Bible Gateway, (2011).

This concludes the *Power of Agape Love as manifested by God who gave us His Only Begotten Son Jesus the perfect sacrifice!* Although we are not perfect, as commissioned by God we must strive for perfection. As Paul quoted in Philippians 3:12 (ISV), "It's not that I have already reached this goal or have already become perfect. But I keep pursuing it, hoping somehow to embrace it just as I have been embraced by the Messiah Jesus." In spreading Agape love to others we are being obedient to God's Word (His commandment), that we love one another as He has loved us (John 15:12). For those of us who know the way, let us remain near to Jesus. To my brothers and sisters who are lost in this darken world, seek Jesus now, for He is the only way.

Without a doubt the enemy of this world aim is to deceive one by giving them a false temporary fixation of contentment. His ultimate aims are to steal, kill, destroy (John 10:10). But *thank God for Jesus*; Our Lord and Savior, who loves you, wants to empower and show you the right way through His Agape love. Agape love is miraculous in offering a buffet of relief from this ailing world and grants one structure, directions, love, peace, joy, contentment, and most importantly eternal life. There is no other way except through Jesus Christ as He informed in His Word, ". . . I am the way and the truth and the life. No one comes to the Father except through me" (John 14:5-6, NIV). I pray "that Christ may dwell in your hearts by faith; that ye, being rooted and grounded in love" (Ephesians 3:17) and His Agape love to others.

-References-

Anapol, D. (November, 2011). Love without limits: Reports from the relationship frontier. *Psychology Today*. Retrieved from https://www.psychologytoday.com/blog/love-without-limits/201111/what-is-love-andwhat-isn't?collection=1070853

Asimov, I. (1988). Asimov's guide to the Bible: Two volumes in one, old and new testaments (reprint ed.). *Wings*. ISBN: 9780517345825.

Baklinski, T. (November, 2013). Principal stops students from saying Lord's prayer in Alberta public school after one complaint. *Life Site News*. Retrieved from https://www.lifesitenews.com/news/principal-stops-students-from-saying-lords-prayer-in-alberta-public-school

Ben-Zeev, A. (September, 2014). Why do (some) men murder the wives they love?: Is killing out of love possible? *Psychology Today*. Retrieved from https://www.psychologytoday.com/blog/in-the-name-love/201409/why-do-some-men-murder-the-wives-they-love

Bergel, G. (1988). Banning prayer in public schools has led to America's demise. *The Forerunner*. Retrieved from http://www.forerunner.com/forerunner/X009 8_Ban_on_school_prayer.html

Berkley, W. E. (January, 1997). It takes a village. *The Expository files.* Mantras of 90's (#1), New series for '97. Retrieved from http://www.bible.ca/ef/topical-it-takes-a-village.htm

Bible Gateway. (2011). Love is greatest: 1 Corinthians 13. Expanded Bible (EXB). *Bible Gateway.* Retrieved from https://www.biblegateway.com/passage/?search=1+Corinthians+13&version=EXB

Brainy Quote. (2015). *Martin Luther King, Jr. Quotes.* Retrieved from http://www.brainyquote.com/quotes/authors/m/martin_luther_king_jr.html

Bromiley, G. M. (1995). "Jezebel." *International Standard Bible Encyclopedia.* Wm. B. Eerdmans Publishing. ISBN: 9780802837820.

Calloway, J. (June, 2013). Restoring the peace (community action day). *Cultural Resources.* Retrieved from http://www.theafricanamericanlectionary.org/PopupCulturalAid.asp?LRID=410

Catron, A. (2015). What is love? A Philosophy of life. *The Huntington Post.* Retrieved from http://www.huffingtonpost.com/adrian-catron/what-is-love-a-philosophy_b_5697322.html

Child Molestation Research & Prevention Institute. (2015). Early diagnoses and effective treatment. *CMRPI.* Retrieved from http://www.childmolestationprevention.org/pages/tell_others_the_facts.html

Chilton, B. (August, 2011). What does the Bible say about the mother of Jesus? *Huffpost Religion.* Retrieved from http://www.huffingtonpost.com/bruce-chilton/mary-mother-of-jesus_b_928333.html

Cobb, J.M. (October, 2005). Hezekiah Walker; 20/85 The experience. *PRAYZEHIM.* Retrieved from http://www.nuthinbutgospel.com/spotlight_h ezekiahwalker.htm

Cooper, P. III, A. (n.d.). The translation of the Greek word "ekklesia" as "church." *The English Bible and its Ramifications.* Retrieved from http://bible-truth.org/Ekklesia.html

DeWitt, J. (September, 2014). Cheerleaders defy school ban on prayer during ACLU-enforced 'moment of silence.' *Top Right News.* Retrieved from http://toprightnews.com/amazing-moment-happens-cheerleaders-defy-school-ban-prayer-aclu-enforced-moment-silence/

Dolan, M. (May, 2013). Father may lose sons if he molests a daughter, court decides. *Los Angeles Times: A Tribune Newspaper Website.* Retrieved from http://www.latimes.com/local/lanow/la-me-ln-father-abuse-20130509-story.html

Doyle, J. (June, 2012). A facebook crime every 40 minutes: From killings to grooming as 12, 300 cases are linked to the site. *Daily Mail.com.* Retrieved from: http://www.dailymail.co.uk/news/article-2154624/A-Facebook-crime-40-minutes-12-

300-cases-linked-site.html

Draper, N. (May, 2013). Mo' money, mo' Problems: Kobe Bryant & other celebrities who sue their parents (photos). *Global Grind.* Retrieved from http://globalgrind.com/news/kobe-bryant-and-other-celebrities-who-sue-their-parents-photos#ixzz2Svw2hhCz

Easton Bible Dictionary. (n.d.). Aaron: Oldest brother of Moses. *Bible Study Notes on Aaron.* Retrieved from ttp://www.biblereferenceguide.com/keywords/aaron.html

Encyclopaedia Britannica (May, 2013). Eros. *Encyclopaedia Britannica Inc.* Retrieved from http://www.britannica.com/EBchecked/topic/191796/Eros

Ewtn. (n.d.). Her words: Quotes of mother Teresa. *EWTN.com.* Retrieved from https://www.ewtn.com/motherteresa/words.htm

Exum, J. C. (2015). Delilah: Bible. *Jewish Women Archive: Encyclopedia.* Retrieved from: http://jwa.org/encyclopedia/article/delilah-bible

Feeding America (2015). The impact of hunger: Hunger and poverty fact sheet. *Feeding America.org.* Retrieved from http://www.feedingamerica.org/hunger-in-america/impact-of-hunger/hunger-and-poverty/hunger-and-poverty-fact-sheet.html?gclid=CIm5jpqXlcgCFQuQaQodAAcKjw?referrer=https://www.google.com/

Ford, D.E. (April, 2015). Racial profiling disorder: Hate groups and domestic terrorism. *Create Space Independent Publishing Platform.*

Gaines, Jr., J. (2015). 1st Corinthians 15:57-58: This is my spot. *ASA Publishing Company.* Monroe, Michigan.

Goad, J. (April, 2014). 20 moms who killed their kids. *Thought Catalog.* Retrieved from http://thoughtcatalog.com/jim-goad/2014/04/20-moms-who-killed-their-kids/

Goodreads. (2015). *Mahatma Gandhi quotes.* Retrieved from http://www.goodreads.com/quotes/41191-prayer-is-not-asking-it-is-a-longing-of-the

Goodreads. (2014). *Martin Luther King Jr. quotes.* Retrieved from http://www.goodreads.com/quotes/29486-love-is-the-only-force-capable-of-transforming-an-enemy

Graves, S. (n.d.). Our testimony. *Time Tracts.* Retrieved from http://timetracts.com/Home/meet-the-graves-2/meet-the-graves/

Greenberg, M. (October, 2012). The 50 best quotes on self-love: Love and appreciate yourself-you're all you have. *Psychology Today: The Mindful Self-Express.* Retrieved from https://www.psychologytoday.com/blog/the-mindful-self-express/201210/the-50-best-quotes-self-love

Guntzelman, J. (2015). Who was blessed mother Teresa? *American Catholic.org.* Retrieved

from
http://www.americancatholic.org/Features/Te
resa/WhoWasTeresa.aspx

Hanson, R. E. (2015). Chapter *10. The internet: Mass communication gets personal.* Retrieved from
http://college.cqpress.com/sites/masscomm/
Home/chapter10.aspx

Harper, C. & McLanahan, S. S. (September, 2004). Father absence and youth incarceration. *Journal of Research on Adolescence 14,* 369-397.

Heaven Questions.com. (2015). *Microchips the mark of the beast: Microchips in humans have become reality.* Retrieved from:
http://heavenquestions.com/MicroChips_-
_The_Mark_of_th.html

Henry, M. (2015a). Matthew Henry Quotes. *Good Reads Incorporation.* Retrieved from
http://www.goodreads.com/author/quotes/91
281.Matthew_Henry?page=4

Henry, M. (2014b). Concise commentary on the whole Bible by Matthew Henry. *Bible Hub.* Retrieved from
http://biblehub.com/commentaries/mhc/1_jo
hn/3.htm

Hirsch, E. G., Price, I. M., Bacher, W., Seligsohn, M., Montgomery, M. W., & Toy, C. H. (2011). Solomon. *JewishEncyclopedia.com. Retrieved from*
http://www.jewishencyclopedia.com/articles/
13842-solomon

Hoffmann, J. P. (May, 2002). The community context of family structure and adolescent drug use. *Journal of Marriage and Family 64:* 314-330.

Howard, K. S., Lefever, J. E.B., Borkowski, J.G., & Whitman, T. L. (2006). Fathers' influence in the lives of children with adolescent mothers. *Journal of Family Psychology, 20*(3), 468–476. Retrieved from http://dx.doi.org/10.1037/0893-3200.20.3.468

KHQ. (May, 2013). Men had pact to kill each other's wives; 3. *The Associated Press.* Retrieved from http://www.khq.com/story/22158240/docum ents-men-had-pact-to-kill-each-others-wives

Kiger, P. J. (February, 2015). Killing Jesus: How did the apostles die? *National Geographic Channel.* Retrieved from http://channel.nationalgeographic.com/killing-jesus/articles/how-did-the-apostles-die/

Lamb, E. (April, 2015). *In devotions, from the author, God's heart.* Retrieved from http://ithoughtiknewwhatlovewas.com/

Laurie, G. (2015). Why did Jesus ask three times if Peter loved Him? *Jesus.org* Retrieved from http://www.jesus.org/life-of-jesus/disciples/why-did-jesus-ask-three-times-if-peter-loved-him.html

Lockyer, H. (August, 2011). All the women of the Bible: Lydia. *Bible Gateway.* Retrieved from https://www.biblegateway.com/devotionals/all-women-bible/2011/08/02

Lucado, M. (February, 2015). *Just like Jesus.* Retrieved from https://maxlucado.com/audio/daily-audio/just-like-jesus/

Ma. (2009). Good morning. *Blogspot.* Retrieved from http://onyama.blogspot.com/2009/01/chapter-1-page-23-book-08.html

Matthews, T.J., Curtin, S. C., & MacDorman, M.F. (2000). Infant mortality statistics from the 1998 period linked birth/Infant death data set. *National Vital Statistics Reports, 48* (12). Hyattsville, MD: National Center for Health Statistics, 2000.

Merriam-Webster (2015a). Love. *Merriam-Webster Incorporated.* Retrieved from http://www.merriam-webster.com/dictionary/love

Merriam-Webster (2015b). Wisdom. *Merriam-Webster: An Encyclopedia Britannica Company.* Retrieved from http://www.merriam-webster.com/dictionary/wisdom

Merriam-Webster (2013). Agape. *Merriam-Webster: An Encyclopedia Britannica Company.* 10. Retrieved from http://www.merriam-webster.com/dictionary/agape

Mills, K. (July, 1994). Husbands kill their spouses more often than wives do. *DeseretNews.com.* Retrieved from http://www.deseretnews.com/article/363824/HUSBANDS-KILL-THEIR-SPOUSES-MORE-OFTEN-THAN-WIVES-DO.html?pg=all

Montaldo, C. (2015a). Profile of Idaho teen killer Sarah Johnson: The murder of Alan and Diane

Johnson. *About News.* Retrieved from
http://crime.about.com/od/current/p/andreay
ates.htm

Montaldo, C. (2015b). Alex and Derek King: How did
he know what you had planned? "It was too
late to play baseball." *About News.* Retrieved
from
http://crime.about.com/od/murder/a/alexand
derekking.htm

National Fatherhood Initiative. (2014). *Father facts:
Statistics on the father absence crisis in
America.* Retrieved from
http://www.fatherhood.org/father-absence-
statistics

New York Call. (2013). Bishop Hezekiah Walker:
Artists. *The New York call: A coalition of
pastors and churches throughout the tri-state
area.* Retrieved from
http://www.nycall.org/hez.html

Nord, C.W., & West, J. (2001). Fathers' and mothers'
involvement in their children's schools by
family type and resident status: (NCES 2001-
032). *Washington, D.C.: U.S. Department of
Education, National Center for Education
Statistics.* Retrieved from
http://eric.ed.gov/?id=ED452982

Open Society Institute. (2010). Closing the addiction
treatment gap: Early accomplishments in a
three year initiative. *Open Society
Foundations.org.* Retrieved from
http://www.opensocietyfoundations.org/sites
/default/files/early-accomplishments-

20100701.pdf

Orenstein, D. (February, 2014). Analysis: 32 years of filicide arrests. Brown University. *News from Brown*. Retrieved from https://news.brown.edu/articles/2014/02/filicide%20

Osborne, C., & McLanahan, S. (2007). Partnership instability and child well-being. *Journal of Marriage and Family 69*, 1065-1083.

Parker, J. (June, 2015). Husband kills wife & children on father's day in triple murder-suicide. *Hollywood Life*. Retrieved from http://hollywoodlife.com/2015/06/22/family-dead-fathers-day-murder-suicide-russell-smith-kills-wife-kids/

Parnell, C. (September, 2015). There are consequences for America's rebellion against God: Part 1. *Newswithviews.com* Retrieved from http://www.newswithviews.com/Parnell/carl1 28.htm

Patel, H. (May, 2015). L.S. Raheja College of arts & commerce. Subject: Media studies. MS media influence project. *Slideshare.net*. Retrieved from: http://www.slideshare.net/himat001patel?ut m_campaign=profiletracking&utm_medium=ss site&utm_source=ssslideview

Paul, V., Singh, P., & Sunita, J. B. (August, 2013). Role of mass media in social awareness. *International Journal of Humanties & Social Science 1*(01). ISBN: 978-93-83006-16-8, 34-

38.
Rosiak, L. (December, 2012). Fathers disappear from households across America. *The Washington Times*. Retrieved from http://www.washingtontimes.com/news/2012/dec/25/fathers-disappear-from-households-across-america/?page=all

Sayings. (n.d.). *Mother Theresa.com* Retrieved from http://mothertheresasayings.com/sayings.htm

Schaefer, G. E. (1996). *Love*. Retrieved from http://www.biblestudytools.cohm/dictionaries/bakers-evangelical-dictionary/love.html

Schmadeke, S. (August, 2011). Bad mothering lawsuit dismissed: Adult children sued mom over birthday cards and college care packages. *Chicago Tribune News*. Retrieved from http://articles.chicagotribune.com/2011-08-28/news/ct-met-mom-sued-0828-20110828_1_mothering-care-packages-birthday-card

Shen, M. (November, 2012). Despite taped confession, accused child molester walks free. *KomoNews.com*. Retrieved from http://www.komonews.com/news/local/When-is-a-taped-confession-of-child-sex-buse-not-enough-for-a-conviction-177702721.html

Skolfield, E. (n.d.). *Introduction-book of revelation*. Retrieved from http://www.bibleprobe.com/revelation.htm

Stewart, D. J. (September, 2012). How much was Delilah paid for betraying Sampson? *Jesus-is-savior.com*. Retrieved from:

http://www.jesus-is-savior.com/Bible/delilah_silver.htm

The Holy Bible. (2012). International Standard Version. *Biblehub.* Retrieved from http://biblehub.com/isv/philippians/3.htm

The Holy Bible. (2011). New International Version (NIV). Romans 15:1-7. *Biblica Incorporation.* Retrieved from https://www.biblegateway.com/passage/?search=Romans%2015:1-7

The Holy Bible. (2001). English Standard Version (ESV). *Bible Gateway.com.* Crossway Bibles: A publishing ministry of Good News Publishers. Retrieved from https://www.biblegateway.com/passage/?search=psalms+41%3A9&version=ESV

The Holy Bible. (1998). King James Version (KJV). Large print compact edition. *Holman Bible Publishers:* Korea.

The Holy Bible. (1982). New King James Version (NKJV). *Bible Gateway.com.* Retrieved from https://www.biblegateway.com/passage/?search=1+Corinthians+13%3A1-8&version=NKJV

The Kim Foundation. (2014). *Statistics: Mental disorders in America.* Retrieved from http://www.thekimfoundation.org/html/about_mental_ill/statistics.html

The Richest. (May, 2015). The most shocking cases of kids who killed their parents. *TheRichest.com.* Retrieved from http://www.therichest.com/rich-list/most-shocking/the-most-shocking-cases-of-kids-who-killed-their-parents/?view=all

U.S. Department of Health & Human Service. (2012). Information on poverty and income statistics: A summary of 2012 current population survey data. Retrieved from https://aspe.hhs.gov/basic-report/information-poverty-and-income-statistics-summary-2012-current-population-survey-data

Valdez, J. (August, 2014). Revelations 2: The beloved church-Ephesus, Smyrna, Pergamun, Thyatira. *Our Great Adventure.* Retrieved from http://www.ourgreatadventure.org/revelation-2-beloved-church/

Wagner, M., & Hensley, N. (August, 2015). Texas man kills ex who once dubbed him 'best father in the whole world, 'her husband, 6 kids: deputies. *New York Daily News.* Retrieved from http://www.nydailynews.com/ne http ws/crime/children-adults-shot-dead-texas-home-report-article-1.2319619

Washington CBS Local. (May, 2015). Survey: Three-quarters of Americans pick mother's day over father's day. *CBS DC.* Retrieved from http://washington.cbslocal.com/2015/05/08/a mericans-pick-mothers-day-over-fathers-day/

Watkins, T. (1999). *Is the biochip the mark of the beast?* Retrieved from http://www.av1611.org/666/biochip.html

Wikipedia. (October, 2015). Internet homicide. *Wikipedia the Free Encyclopedia.* Retrieved

from
https://en.wikipedia.org/wiki/Internet_homici
de

Wikipedia. (July, 2015). Wisdom. *Wikipedia the Free Encyclopedia.* Retrieved from https://en.wikipedia.org/wiki/Wisdom

Wikipedia. (May, 2015). Engel v. Vitale. *Wikipedia the Free Encyclopedia.* Retrieved from http://en.wikipedia.org/wiki/Engel_v._Vitale

Wikipedia. (November, 2014). Score. *Wikipedia the Free Encyclopedia.* Retrieved from https://simple.wikipedia.org/wiki/Score

Wikipedia (May, 2013). Storge. *Wikipedia the Free Encyclopedia.* Retrieved from http://en.wikipedia.org/wiki/Storge

Word Press. (2014). Quote investigator: Exploring the origins of quotations. If you don't stand for something, you'll fall for anything. *Quoteinvestigator.com* Retrieve from http://quoteinvestigator.com/2014/02/18/sta nd-fall/

Wybourne, C. (2015). What is Love? Five theories on the greatest emotion of all. *The Guardian.* Retrieved from http://www.theguardian.com/commentisfree/ 2012/dec/13/what-is-love-five-theories

Zavada, J. (May, 2013). What is Philia? Philia Love in the Bible. *About.com. Christianity.* Retrieved from http://christianity.about.com/od/glossary/a/P hilia.htm